WILD CANARY

WILD CANARY

By C.K. Thompson, R.A.O.U., J.P.

(Member of the Royal Australasian Ornithologists' Union)

This edition published 2017
By Living Book Press
147 Durren Rd, Jilliby, 2259
Copyright © The Estate of C.K. Thompson, 1956

The publisher would like to give a huge 'Thank You' to the author's family for their assistance in making this book available once more.

National Library of Australia Cataloguing-in-Publication entry:

Creator:	Thompson, C.K. (Charles Kenneth), 1904-1980 author
Title:	Old Bob's birds / C.K. Thompson
ISBN:	9780648104827 (paperback)
Target Audience:	For primage school age.
Subjects:	Canaries--Australia--Juvenile fiction.
	Canaries--Juvenile fiction.

CONTENTS

DEDICATION

To my good friend, MISS NOLA WILLIAMS, of Teralba, N.S.W. whose terrific energy on the golf course would leave the most active canary breathless, and for whom my personal regard alone prevents me from smashing my recording of Smoky Mokes."

FOREWORD

During the disastrous floods that swept the Hunter Valley of N.S.W. during February 1955, an old friend of mine who lived just out of the danger zone, saw five canaries in his backyard one morning. They were feeding off some pieces of stale bread my friend had thrown out for the local sparrows. He could not catch them, and presently they flew away. Where they had come from and what happened to them eventually, nobody can tell, though one can hazard a rough guess.

It was that rather sorrowful episode, together with another that I have mentioned elsewhere in this book, that inspired me to write this saga of a free canary.

When a canary escapes from a cage, what are its chances of prolonged existence in a world filled with deadly perils for even the hardy, bush-wise birds, hatched and reared in complete freedom? Canaries are the development of Man. They have no native initiative, no inborn experience, no instinctive knowledge upon which to rely. They are at the mercy of everyone and everything. By the very nature of its breeding, a canary has small chance of living out its normal life span outside the protection of its cage, but with a great deal of luck—and it would have to be exceptional luck—it *might* make it. Who can tell? Even the most experienced ornithologist cannot claim to know everything about every bird. Given a fair chance, might not a canary be able to relearn the native lore bred out of him by Man?

I should mention that none of the episodes in this book had any parallel, as far as I am aware, during the 1955 Hunter River floods. The names of the human characters are purely fictitious, and if I have inadvertently mentioned the name of a living person, it is purely coincidental and certainly not deliberate. I definitely would not run the risk of having any of my old friends and former fellow-townspeople of Maitland (where I was born) seeking me out, thirsting for my blood!

C. K. THOMPSON.

CHAPTER ONE

Flood Threat

IT had been raining steadily for over a week, and more than one farmer in the valley had shaken his head despondently. It was flood rain, and every one of them knew it.

That river valley had been devastated by floods before even the first white settlers, lured by the promise of better land beyond the distant horizon, had battled their way through bush and scrub with their assigned convict servants, to carve for themselves a home on the rich land agriculturally unappreciated by the wandering aboriginal tribes whose hunting ground it was.

That had been more than one hundred years ago. The valley now was covered with prosperous farming settlements on land that could produce almost every kind of crop known to man. Seasons, uniformly, were good.

Certainly there had been poor years when the rainfall was below average, but these invariably were followed by many bountiful times—years which made the valley one of the most prosperous in the whole of Australia.

But periodically came the floods, and farmers who deemed themselves most fortunate saw, in a few soul-shaking days, the wealth and labour perhaps of years, swept away—submerged, wrecked and ruined under a fast-moving torrent of swirling flood water.

They clung, however, tenaciously to their land, as their fathers before them had done. It was their home and their heritage, and nothing could change the mode of living that tradition and inclination had made a very part of them.

It was thoughts such as these that occupied the mind of John Westwood as he sat with his wife, his small son and small daughter in the family kitchen that night, listening to the persistent drumming of the rain upon the farmhouse roof. The latest reports on the radio had been that the river in its upper reaches was rising fast, and that the lower valley could expect big floods. Residents of all low-lying land had already been advised to move.

"I just can't see why we should have to shift," Westwood said to his wife. "After all, we have been through floods before and we have made out all right. They're making a mountain out of a molehill."

"We lost nearly everything we possessed last flood, John," Mrs. Westwood pointed out. "The whole of our crops were ruined and so was most of our furniture. We could have saved that if we had got out in time."

"Yes, if we had got out in time," retorted her husband. "We didn't. The river was inside the back door before we knew it was over the bank."

"That was before they installed the radio flood warning system," said Mrs. Westwood. "The regular reports they put out now tell us everything we want to know and well in advance. They reported only half an hour ago that this was going to be a record flood, and that everyone should move to higher ground before the water from up-river reached here. I think we should pack up and go. I for one do not want to spend another night in that hayshed loft as we did in the last flood because we were too pigheaded to move."

John Westwood looked obstinate.

"I'm not pig-headed and you can go if you want to," he said. "I'm sticking by the house. I can't shift it and the farm with it. I can't sweep back the river with a broom as King Canute did with the sea."

"He didn't do that, dad," put in young 12-years-old Jack

Westwood. "He tried to order the sea to go back, but it didn't work."

"It wouldn't work with me, either, my lad," said his father.

"I'll stick by you, John," said his wife, "but I think you should take the children to safety. It is not fair to risk their lives."

"Who's risking anyone's lives?" exclaimed the farmer. "I won't have it said that I risked the lives of my family! All I'm saying is that the false-alarmists over the radio are scaring people into leaving their homes when there isn't sufficient cause."

"Now how can you possibly say that? You are here in one spot in the lower valley, while the reports are coming in from all over the place. Those people would not put out scare stories. The reports are coming from the police and the Local Government authorities. They are not scare-mongers."

"Our teacher said at school today that the river is so silted up that even a little bit of rain can cause a flood, because the bed of the stream is not deep enough to carry away all the water," remarked young Mary.

"So the school teachers are in it, too, with their panic talk," snorted the farmer. He looked sternly at his ten-years-old daughter.

"It is time you were in bed," he said. "That goes for your brother, too."

"But it's only eight o'clock, dad!" exclaimed the girl. "We'd like to stay up and listen to the flood bulletins on the wireless."

John Westwood groaned aloud. "Flood bulletins! Flood warnings! That's all I hear from morning to night!" he complained. "We are nearly two miles from the river and it is not yet a banker. Added to that, there are the embankments between us and the stream. It would take the father of all floods to reach us here now."

"It has happened before, John," said his wife. "I think you are being just plain obstinate. We can't do any good by staying here. I think we should pack up and go as soon as we can. We can easily load our furniture on to the lorry and take it to my sister's place on the hill. We could shift the lot in a couple of trips."

"And what about the horses and the cows? Your sister won't want them cluttering up her backyard."

"They can be turned loose on the high ground. In a state of emergency like this, maybe the council won't impound them."

Westwood pondered the matter, irresolute. He realised that there was a great deal of common sense in his wife's argument, but he was disinclined to leave the property. He turned the matter over in his mind and decided to compromise.

"We will wait and see what the morning brings," he said. "If things look bad then, we can discuss the question of getting out."

He stood up and yawned. Outside the wind howled mournfully and the patter of rain on the roof went on unceasingly.

"I'm half-inclined to drive across to the bridge and see what the river-height gauge says," he remarked. "I might also hear some late news from up-river."

"May I come with you, dad?" asked young Jack eagerly.

"Your place is in bed," replied his father. "See that you are between the blankets before I get back from the bridge. Oh, and by the way. Why is that bird-cage hanging on the wall? Didn't I tell you to leave it outside on the verandah? That useless canary makes more mess than he is worth. He's always chucking seed over the floor and splashing the place with water when he has a bath. Outside is the place for him."

"It's too wet on the verandah tonight, dad," protested the boy. "Anyway, his cage is covered up and he can't throw seed out."

"That bird could throw seed through a Russian Iron Curtain," retorted his father. He shot a half-annoyed glance at the covered canary cage hanging on the wall a few feet away.

"Oh, leave the kids and their pet alone, John," said Mrs. Westwood impatiently. "The canary isn't doing any harm there. And it is too cold and wet outside for him. Don't make a song and dance about nothing!"

"It's not too cold and wet outside for the cows and horses and fowls," retorted the farmer. "Do you suggest that we bring them all into the house and make a menagerie out of the place?"

"You're just talking rubbish now. Horses and cows and fowls are different," said Mrs. Westwood. "The fowls are in a covered shed and the animals are used to being out in all weathers. Leave the canary alone and go across to the bridge to see the river height, if you are going to."

"But it's such a ratbag of a bird," went on the farmer, taking no notice of his wife's remarks. "It won't whistle if you look at it, or if it is whistling and it sees you looking at it, it stops. Instead of sitting on a perch and eating its seed from the tin like a sensible bird, it clings to the wire and eats upside down. It lies in a corner of the cage in the sun like a dog having a snooze. Did you ever hear of such a stupid boofhead?"

"He isn't stupid at all; he's just sensitive," said young Mary. "And don't call him Boofhead. It's such a silly name."

"A silly name for a silly bird," nodded her father. He then left the room in search of his oilskins and knee boots.

Mary went over to the cage and, gently lifting a corner of the cloth that covered it, gazed affectionately at the yellow ball crouched on a perch in the corner. "Boofhead," quite unconscious of the criticism so recently levelled at him, was fast asleep, his head buried in the soft feathers of his right wing. He had no worries. A tin of seed, a frequent thistle, an occasional apple core, drinking water and a dish in which to have a bath-—give him these and life had nothing more to offer. In return, he filled the farmhouse with gay song all day long—providing nobody looked at him too closely.

For Boofie, although, like all healthy canaries, he took a keen and lively interest in everything that went on around him, was a trifle shy. He detested anyone fooling around with his cage, even the Westwood children. He should have known that they would do him no harm, but he was in a state of panic every time his cage was cleaned out or his seed and water changed. Such a fluttering from perch to perch, a frantic clinging to cage wires and protesting chirps ensued, that an onlooker would have gained the impression that an attempt was being made to murder him.

In appearance, Boofie was undistinguished. Plain yellow, with one black spot as big as threepence on the back of his head and a touch of buff on his right wing, he was of that popular breed known as Border Fancy.

The Westwoods had had him for two years, and, in spite of Mr. Westwood's criticisms, the whole family was attached to him.

"Old floods do not worry you, do they, boy?" asked Mary softly. The yellow ball made no reply. The little girl blew gently, causing the feathers to ruffle slightly. Then she blew a little harder and out of the fluffed-up plumage shot a small head, bright little eyes regarding her with some indignation. Mary did not move, and Boofie, having opened and closed his beak three times, plunged his head back into his shoulder feathers. The game, as far as he was concerned, was over. Mary smiled at him and returned to her seat.

At this moment her father entered the room, clad in thick oilskins and wearing an ancient felt hat. Outside the wind howled louder and the rain drummed on roof and windows like a hail of gunshot.

"I shouldn't be long, mother," he told his wife. "I'll have a look at the river gauge and see if I can pick up any information about the up-river rain. I really don't think we have anything to worry about, though."

"I hope not, John," she replied. "Still, it is better to be sure than to be sorry. Look after yourself, my dear."

"I'll do that, never fear, old girl," said the farmer, and kissed her.

Mrs. Westwood accompanied him to the door and quickly closed it against the howling elements as he disappeared into the rain-swept night.

CHAPTER TWO

Flood Refugees

THE Westwood farmhouse lay about a mile and a half from the river bank and on its eastern side. On the western bank stood the township, the main street of which followed the meanderings of the stream in an irregular curve for perhaps half a mile. The town was on a higher level than the farms, but the curve in the stream caused the floodwater continually to dash its great force against the western bank. The authorities were alive to the fact that should the rising torrent sweep away the embankment and take a straight course through the town instead of rounding the bend, disaster would be swift and terrible.

Hour by hour the water rose and it was quite apparent by the morning that nothing could prevent a most disastrous flood. This was brought home even to the stubborn John Westwood, whose visit the previous night to the river gauge on the bridge that spanned the stream between farmlands and township, had convinced him that he must remove his family and household goods as quickly as possible.

As he could see no sense in having the two children remain at home that day, he sent them off to school as usual, with instructions not to return home that afternoon, but to go to their aunt's home on the high ground outside the town.

With the children safely out of the way, he set to work energetically to "shift camp," as he put it. Westwood owned a big motor lorry, and he and his wife spent the whole of the morning packing their movable household goods and, with the help of a couple of neighbours, loading them on to the vehicle. He made trip after trip to the aunt's home and by early afternoon the whole job was completed, a fact that caused Mrs. Westwood to sigh with relief. Horses and cattle and fowls were removed to safety and now the floods could do their worst! It was a source of satisfaction that the rain had eased off, but the gravity of the situation was increasing every minute. Already the river was over its banks in several places, and a lot of low-lying land had been inundated. The Westwood farmhouse, however, was still untouched, as were a number of other homes in the same area.

It was this fact that persuaded Westwood, when his own job was done, to place his lorry and his own services at the disposal of his friends and neighbours.

Darkness was falling as the last load of furniture was transported to safety and Westwood drove off with a light heart to rejoin his family at their relations' home. The evening meal was on the table when he arrived and he announced heartily that he could eat a horse. He was immediately provided with a large meal.

It was a subdued family that sat around the table that night. Mr. and Mrs. Grahame (Uncle Bert and Auntie Maude) and the four Westwoods sensed the tragedy in the air and they all knew, even the children, that terrible events were going to happen.

"We can thank God that we are safe," said Uncle Bert. "But I fear for the families who have not moved from the low land. And if the town embankment gives away . . ." He paused significantly and was silent.

"Er, I hope your fowlhouse isn't too crowded, Bert," said Westwood, bridging an awkward gap in the conversation. "It's pretty full now of birds, what with yours and all mine."

"It won't hurt 'em to rough it for a few days," said Grahame. "They're all tough birds."

"You've said it!" exclaimed Westwood. "I find that out every time I kill one for Sunday dinner!"

That raised a laugh, a laugh which was stilled when young Mary gave a subdued scream.

"Birds! Birds!" she cried out. "Oh, dear!"

"What's wrong with you, girl?" demanded her father. "Been bitten by a bull-ant?"

"Boofie!" the girl cried. "Boofie! Where's Boofie?"

"Boofie? Who on earth is Boofie?" asked Auntie Maude.

"My canary!" cried Mary, bursting into tears. "Where is he? Oh, daddy, you forgot all about him! Oh, he's left all alone in the house and I know he'll be drowned."

"Oh, my gosh! I did forget all about him!" muttered Westwood. "As far as I know, he's still in the cage hanging on the kitchen wall. How in the name of heaven did I manage to leave him behind when we were doing all the shifting today?"

"Please save poor Boofie, daddy," wept Mary, who was now joined in her lamentations by her brother Jack.

"Listen, I'm tired out and it's raining cats and dogs outside," protested their father. "It's a long way back to the farmhouse. I'll get him in the morning. Maybe the flood won't reach him . . . "

"Stop it, John," his wife cut in sharply. "Don't make things worse. You know that the farmhouse won't be flooded at all." She gave him a good kick on the shin beneath the table and he shut up abruptly.

"Oh, of course he'll be as safe as the bank," he said with spurious heartiness. "I'll pop over first thing in the morning and collect the old chap."

"You'll pop over right now, John," said Mrs. Westwood quietly. "He is the children's pet and it's your fault that he is still at the farm."

"How do you make that out?" demanded the farmer. "Never mind answering that. Naturally I'm to blame for everything that happens around the place. It has always been the same. But as for going over there at this time of the night in the rain to get him, I'm not that nutty."

"You'll go over right now, John, or there will be a first-class row," said his wife sharply.

"Okay, okay, but get off my back, will you?" grunted Westwood. He could not understand all the fuss over a worthless canary which, in any case, would probably be safe until the morning. But he would have to go and rescue the thing or he'd never hear the end of it. Ah, well, it would be a chance to have a last look round the farmhouse and see what its chances were of escaping destruction.

Bert Grahame offered to accompany him for the ride, but the farmer would not hear of it. "One goat is enough out in this weather," he snorted as he left the house. Within a few minutes he had the lorry on the road and was driving swiftly towards the township.

When he reached the bridge he stopped the lorry and spoke to one of a group of men who, huddled up in raincoats and knee boots, were anxiously watching the debris-laden torrent of swirling water rushing swiftly under the structure.

"Yes, mate," said the man in answer to Westwood's query, "she's still rising. Another few feet and the bridge decking will be under water."

"H'm, that doesn't sound so hot," mused the farmer. "Embankments still holding?"

"So far. The gangs are working on all of them, strengthening them with sandbags. The trouble is, it's still raining heavily upstream, and all that water's got to come down, you know. Guess we'll all be floating out to sea by morning." He laughed shortly, but there was no mirth in the laugh.

"Any reports from the farms over the river?" asked Westwood.

"Nothing new. They've all shifted off the flat, at least that's what I've heard. Of course, there might still be a few mugs left— you know the sort, mate: the dills who think the flood won't reach their places and the other ratbags who insist on sticking to their homes, come floods, fires or atom bombs. They're an utter nuisance. They put their own lives in peril and also force other people to risk theirs to rescue them."

Westwood did not answer that. The thought occurred to him that only for his family's persistence he himself might have been classed among the "dills," the "mugs" and the "ratbags."

"My place is over on the flats," he said. "It's about a mile or so from here and I'm just slipping over to pick up the last bit of stuff."

"Take my advice, mate, and don't risk it," said the man earnestly. "The river is over its banks in some spots and the flats might even now be under water. Fair dinkum, I wouldn't risk it if I were you. Matter of fact, the police will turn you back if they spot you."

"I can't see any of them around," said Westwood. "I'll take a chance on it. A man can always turn around and come back if he runs into trouble."

"Yes, unless one of the embankments happens to go while you're over there," said the man darkly.

Cheerful cove, that, Westwood told himself as he drove across the bridge. It was a stout structure that had withstood many assaults by the river in the thirty years it had been standing, but the force of the waters of this Old Man flood beating against its piles caused it to shudder and tremble. Westwood felt it as the lorry rattled across. "Don't try to make it unless it is urgent," that man back there had said. Urgent? What would the fellow have said, Westwood thought with a grim smile, had he known that this crazy trip in the howling dark was to rescue one undistinguished canary—a bird that would throw the judges into fits if anyone were silly enough to exhibit it in a bird show.

At the other side of the bridge there was another group of people anxiously watching the river and discussing the possibilities. He did not speak to them nor take any notice of their hails, but drove steadily onwards. A few hundred yards the other side of the bridge he swung to the left and followed a good road for a quarter of a mile. This brought him to the track that led to his own house. There was a rather deep dip here, a depression that ran at right angles to the river, and it was filled with water. Westwood stopped the lorry, leaving the headlights on, and tested the water with a stick. It was a foot deep and visibly rising. If that depression were completely filled it would be three feet under in the middle impossible for his truck to cross. At the rate the water was rising this should not happen for half an hour or more—time enough for him to rescue the canary and return home to Uncle Bert's place.

Back in the lorry, he splashed across the depression and soon was rattling towards the farmhouse. It looked wet and forlorn in the darkness.

Stopping the lorry outside the back door, Westwood jumped down and quickly made his way into the kitchen. Switching on the light, he saw, sure enough, the open-wire cage hanging on the wall. Inside, head buried in his shoulder feathers, squatted Boofie, sleeping the sleep of the untroubled.

"Come on, you fool bird, we've got no time to waste hanging around here," said the farmer, and lifted the cage from the wall. The movement awakened the canary, which fluttered from perch to perch in its excitement.

"This isn't the time for you to be putting on your act, Boofhead," admonished Westwood. "Calm down and let us get out of here, unless you want to go floating down the river."

He was walking towards the door when a thought occurred to him.

"I'd better have a look around the place before I leave," he told the indignant canary. "There might be something we left behind this afternoon."

Still carrying the cage, he walked from room to room, switching lights on and off as he did so. Except for a few odds and ends of no value, the place was bare. Everything had been removed that day.

"Okay, Boofhead, let's go," he said briskly. "We'd better be getting back to Uncle Bert's. The kids will be anxious, I know, about your precious safety."

Putting out the kitchen light, he left the house, closing and locking the door behind him. Climbing into the lorry, he placed the cage on the seat at his side. Boofie, of course, objected to the whole proceedings and did a bit of fluttering around the cage and acrobatics on the perches to indicate that fact. His attitude showed quite plainly that he thought it was a bit thick. Why couldn't a decent, respectable canary, who did no harm to anyone, be allowed to catch up on his sleep? What was the idea of dragging him around the countryside at dead of night in wind and rain and flood?

It was just as well for Boofie that he did not know just how little sleep he was going to catch up on that particular night!

Westwood received his first warning that all was not as he hoped it would be, when he got to within a hundred yards of the water-filled depression. In the glare of the headlights he saw water where it had no right to be. He had estimated that it would take at least half an hour for the depression to fill completely; yet, within a bare ten minutes, not only was the depression filled, but it was actually flowing over—and fast. He stopped the lorry, got out and ran towards the approaching water. It swirled around his feet and rushed on towards the lorry behind him. This was serious! What could have happened? He thought quickly. It could mean but one thing—the embankment had given way and the river itself was pouring into the depression, turning it into a creek that would run right through the farmlands and quickly inundate them completely.

It was impossible for him to cross the water in the lorry and there was no other road back to the township. Westwood realised that he was marooned—trapped by the rising floodwaters with no chance of reaching safety, at least before morning, and that was many hours away.

By this time the water was up to his ankles. And above the sound of the rain that was falling again steadily and relentlessly, he could hear the dull roar of the racing river, a substantial portion of which was swiftly covering his farm in an ever-deepening flood.

Squelching through the water which was running into the tops of his boots, Westwood reached the lorry, started the engine, and backed until he could turn. Then he drove headlong back to the farmhouse, the tyres sending cascades of water outwards like the bows of miniature steamers. He beat the water to the house, but only just. For as he leaped to the ground it caught up with him.

The farmer was in a dilemma. He knew that he could not stay on the sodden ground. The flood water was racing across the flat to rejoin the river where the bend straightened out. There it would encounter another embankment and would back up swiftly. That meant that as long as the embankment held, the water would continue to rise and rise fast. He had to reach the highest peak he could. Swiftly he looked at the homestead and then at the hayshed. The hayshed it was. There was a ladder inside that led up to a loft from which a trapdoor gave access to the flat platform on which was installed a small block and tackle set used for lifting bales of hay and stowing them on to trucks in the lucerne season. This platform was twenty feet from the ground and he should be safe there. No flood in the history of the valley had ever reached that height!

Westwood acted quickly. Pausing only long enough to grab an electric torch from the lorry seat, he rushed into the hayshed and quickly scaled the ladder. Opening the trapdoor, he emerged on to the platform in the wind and rain. Visibility was not too good, and as he could see no sense in getting wet unnecessarily, he retreated into the loft again. He would be safe there until the morning. He might even get a little sleep. There was a bundle of hay on the floor and that would make a sufficient bed. The absence of a light would not trouble him. He had his flashlight for eventualities.

"All for the sake of a useless canary," he muttered. "What a mug a man can be!" Suddenly he gasped. That canary! Where was it? Oh, starve the lizards, it was still down there in the lorry!

Switching on the torch, Westwood shone it down the ladder and what he saw appalled him. Already there was over a foot of water tearing through the shed. He would have to hurry. Stowing the torch in his overcoat pocket, he quickly shinned down the ladder and landed with a splash into the water—to be almost swept off his feet. The lorry was only a yard or two away and he managed to reach it, but only by throwing himself at it and grabbing the edge of the table-top with one hand while he held the lighted torch in the other. He edged his way along to the driver's door, wrenched it open and hauled himself inside, collapsing on the seat alongside Boofie's cage. He paused for a moment to get his breath back and then got ready for the return journey. He would have to make this without the aid of the flashlight. He could not carry the cage in one hand and the torch in the other. He would need one hand free to steady and guide himself.

It was as dark as pitch, and though he could not see Boofie, he could hear him. The canary was once again registering its protests against this night filled with such unprecedented occurrences, by fluttering around the cage.

Westwood stepped gingerly into the rising water and had to keep a firm grasp on to the door of the lorry to prevent himself being swept away. The hayshed ladder was only a few feet off, but he was going to have a hard job reaching it .

Facing the flow of the stream, he edged himself sideways, inch by inch, the water tearing at his legs, trying to hurl him over. Bit by bit he progressed and bit by bit he won his way. It was with a grunt of thankfulness that his free hand touched the ladder and then it took him only a few seconds to scale it and reach the safety of the loft.

Placing the cage on top of an old kerosene case, he produced his torch and shone it upon Boofie. That ungrateful bird eyed him balefully. It was sitting on the end of a perch as far away from Westwood's side of the cage as it could get. Its look said, quite plainly, that it did not like Westwood. At that moment Westwood did not like Boofie, and did not hesitate to tell him so. Boofie opened and closed his beak three times in complete contempt, and then shoved his head into his shoulder feathers to indicate that the episode was concluded. Westwood put out the torch and sought the heap of hay in the corner.

It was, of course, at this stage, quite impossible for him to go to sleep. The night was not very cold, but he was practically wet through. His clothes clung to his body, causing discomfort, but it was not that that worried him. His thoughts were with his family. Admittedly, they were safely beyond reach of the flood, but as the night wore on and he failed to return home, they would become very worried and anxious. Possibly they would not expect him home immediately. No doubt they would, in the early stages, attribute his absence to a desire to remain in the township to gather the latest news and to render assistance in the thousand and one tasks that could be found for an able-bodied man in such times of distress; but as the hours passed they could not fail to be overcome by worry.

Westwood stirred restlessly on his heap of hay and at length decided to inspect his surroundings. The rain, which had eased off temporarily, had started again and was drumming ceaselessly upon the iron roof just over his head.

Emerging on to the platform, he looked towards the township, the lights of which were faintly visible through the mist caused by the rain. He saw the lights reflected in a vast sea of hurrying water. Glancing downwards, he could still see the roof of the farmhouse, but of his lorry there was no sign. Hastily he pulled the torch from his pocket and directed its strong beam down towards where the thought the vehicle would be standing. It was not there. Or, if it still stood where he had parked it, it was now completely submerged and invisible.

"At the rate this is going on," he told himself grimly, "the water will be up here and I'll be swimming before morning."

Retreating to the shelter of the loft, he again sought the heap of hay, and as he sat down, shone the torch at the canary cage. Boofie was still fast asleep. Vaguely, the farmer resented the bird's innocent detachment and felt inclined to wake it up. Then he shrugged his shoulders and began to brood to himself in the darkness.

And so the time passed slowly. Presently Westwood began to nod. It had been a long and tiring day and he felt exhausted.

Suddenly he was jerked into wakefulness by a resounding crash, to find the shed quivering as if something had struck it heavily. He blinked his eyes a few times and then there was another crash. Something *had* struck the shed! Driftwood, probably, but by the force of the impact it must have been a full-sized tree.

With his torch flashing, he went out on to the platform. The rain had eased off again, but visibility was still poor.

Westwood was appalled by what he saw. The floodwater was within two feet of the very platform on which he stood. And as he watched, he noticed coming towards him out of the night, borne on the turbulent, racing water, an enormous dark object. He could not make out what it was for a few seconds; but when it got nearer he saw that it was a house, or a substantial portion of it; and what was more, unless some quirk of the current changed its course very promptly, it was going to barge into the hayshed right at the point where he now stood.

The farmer turned and rushed into the loft, to cower into the furthest corner. With his breath held tightly and his body braced to withstand the shock, he awaited the impact, praying that the flood-borne dwelling would miss the shed. It didn't. There was a loud crash and the sound of rending timbers, and Westwood found himself flat on the floor of the loft, while the whole shed shook and trembled. From outside came the sound of tearing and bumping as if the derelict were disintegrating and sweeping around the shed. Westwood, his heart beating madly, stayed where he was on the loft floor until the noise died away and nothing was to be heard save the monotonous roaring of the waters.

It was quite five minutes before he felt up to venturing out onto the platform again and then nothing but the raging flood greeted him. Far away across the torrent he could still see the lights of the township. Then suddenly they went out. Unless the council authorities had switched them off for some safety purpose, the floodwaters must have entered the powerhouse itself. This was near the centre of the town, and if it were flooded then the main town embankment had been breached.

Westwood felt like weeping aloud. What hope was there now for the thousands of people who lived there? They would be drowned and their homes swept away. No human endeavour could prevent that catastrophe.

It was at this point in his lamentations over the troubles of other people that he became urgently aware of his own particular peril. He felt a slight tug at his boots and, glancing down, saw that the water was swirling over the platform. He would have to shift, and shift right speedily. But where was he to shift to? The highest point was the roof of the shed itself, but how in the name of fortune was he to reach that? The pitch of the galvanised iron was not steep, thank goodness, but it was wet and smooth and how he was going to negotiate it, at the same time carrying a canary cage, he just did not know. If it came to the last desperate point he would have to abandon Boofie to the flood and try to save himself. That was all there was to it.

He had little or no hope of rescue. With the township itself in the grip of the torrent, everyone would have his own life to save. There would be no time to think of strays like him. The crushing truth was that not a soul knew he was there. The people on the bridge had seen him drive across—hadn't he spoken to some of them —but who would spare a thought for him in the midst of their own troubles? Not a soul. No, people would be wholly preoccupied with their own perils, not those of a fool who had risked his life to save a silly canary.

There was the possibility of the hayshed itself being demolished by the fierce current, but Westwood did not anticipate that happening. It was empty and enclosed on only two sides. Possibly some of the wood and iron with which it was built would go, but the huge supporting uprights would stand. And as long as they stood, the loft itself was safe.

By the light of the torch he consulted his watch. It was three o'clock in the morning. Dawn would not come for about two hours.

It was then that he realised that the water was not rising. He flashed his torch around the loft and saw that there were two inches of water running over the floor, but it was not getting higher. He decided not to make a move yet towards trying to gain the roof. Perhaps the water would drop, and he would not have to make the attempt.

There was nothing he could do. He was cooped up in that loft with Boofie, who was still sleeping peacefully. He had, of course, been awakened when the derelict house had struck the shed, but, in his reckoning, that had happened long since. Westwood decided to wait patiently until the morning and hope that some miracle would deliver him up to rescuers.

Lifting the cage, he sat down on the kerosene case and placed the cage on his knees. Grimly he determined to sit it out. He could do nothing more. If the flood rose higher he would have to abandon Boofie and trust to his own swimming prowess to get him somewhere.

"And that won't be very far," he told Boofie dolefully.

It was just before daybreak that the water began to rise again. Westwood could feel it creeping up his legs.

It was a murky, misty, menacing dawn of leaden skies and vast seas of sullen, yellow water, which raced past the shed, bearing on its treacherous bosom all kinds of pitiful debris—logs, trees, the carcases of drowned birds and beasts, now and then a haystack, a shed, a bit of furniture . . . and other things.

Westwood could not see the slightest hope for either himself or Boofie. This was the end. He had no way of reaching the roof, so had to stay where he was and go out as bravely as he could. Well, he was an Australian, and he would die game. His thoughts turned to his family and there were tears in his eyes, tears he did not try to control.

Now it was daylight, and he could see the full extent of the flood. He could also see that the water was almost to his knees. Carrying the fluttering Boofie in his cage, he waded to the loft opening, but did not venture out on to the platform. It would be foolhardy to step out on it. He might miss his footing and be swept off his balance.

"Well, Boofhead, old timer," he said to that ruffled bird. "This looks like the end of the road. There is little chance for me, but I'm not going to see you drowned like a rat in a trap, or rather, a bird in a cage. I'm going to give you a sporting chance. It's a pretty long shot and the odds are against you, but you might make out. You've got wings, that's one thing. It's a long flight for you, and you're not used to flying, but it's your only chance. Give it a go, old boy."

Opening the cage door with his free hand, he groped for the canary. Boofie did not assist him, of course. He fluttered madly around the cage, eluding the clutching fingers.

"Oh, for heaven's sake, don't go acting the nanny goat now," groaned the farmer. "What a time to be putting on your fool act!"

He made a sudden and determined grab at the canary, which had crouched in a corner on the floor of the cage, and succeeded in imprisoning it in his hand. Dropping the cage, which disappeared into the flood, Westwood, with some emotion, gazed at the little yellow head, with its bright, beady eyes, poking out of his clenched fist.

"Goodbye, old lad, and all the best. You'll need it!" he said. Then, holding out his arm at full length, he slowly opened his hand. For a second the bird just lay on his palm and then it made a sudden dart into the air. Straight out over the swirling waters it shot and then, as if in stark bewilderment, doubled round and disappeared over Westwood's head and out of his sight.

"Good luck!" the man shouted. "Wish me the same!"

And good luck did come Westwood's way; for not five minutes after he had released the canary, one of those famous army amphibious vehicles, known far and wide affectionately as "Duck," rescued him. The crew of keen-faced, but grim and tired-eyed young soldiers, battling around the floodwaters in search of strays such as he, saw Westwood's frantic signals, splashed over to the shed, picked him up and transported him to safety.

CHAPTER THREE

An Ancient Mariner

BOOFIE, perched precariously on the ridge-capping of the hayshed, literally did not know where he was. The sudden transition from the narrow confines of a wire cage to the complete freedom of the world at large, was something that his small bird brain could not assimilate. Even when he had been released from Westwood's hand and had flown away he had expected to hit the wires of his cage, and though he had encountered no such obstacle, it had been the instinctive feeling that he would that had made him wheel sharply round and shoot skywards, to come to rest on the peak of the roof. It was not a good enough perch by any means—he could not grasp anything. But it was wide enough for him to stand on, and that was something.

Boofie was hungry. He had had nothing to eat for many hours. The cage had contained some seed when Westwood had first taken it off the kitchen wall, but since then the many jostlings and bumps had got rid of everything, including both seed and water bottles on either side of the cage.

He made a few attempts to sing, but it seemed silly in the circumstances, so he commenced to preen himself. It was a foolish thing to attempt, because he had no clawgrasp, and when he stood on one leg and stretched out a wing with the other, he lost his balance and went sliding down the sloping roof. He had almost reached the swirling water before he recovered and managed to get into the air. He did not return to the ridge-capping, but set a course, rather aimlessly, straight across the flood, his darting, undulating flight being rather awkward. Until a few minutes previously he had never flown more than two feet in the whole of his life.

Fifty yards from the shed the top of a big gum tree protruded from the torrent, and Boofie made for this. He just got there. In the tree were three sparrows, wet and bedraggled objects, who had spent the whole of the previous night there in the rain. Naturally perky and aggressive, the sparrows at the moment were feeling sick and sorry for themselves. They were on a lower branch than that on which Boofie had alighted, and they were as hungry as he was, with not the slightest idea where their next meal was coming from—or when. They had gone to roost in that tree at dusk on the previous night, with conditions practically normal. It had been raining, of course, but that was nothing. Before going to sleep they had seen all the old familiar scenes—the farmlands and the Westwood house around which they had often scavenged most satisfactorily—but dawn had revealed a startling transformation.

Up in their tree they were like three small, wet-feathered Ancient Mariners, with water, water everywhere. But whereas the original Ancient Mariner had seen water, water everywhere, and not a drop to drink, the sparrows had plenty to drink but nothing to eat. The nearest land was a mile and a half away and as yet they had not attempted to reach it. The non-stop flight would not be too much for those hardy birds, and in any case there were plenty of resting places in between—tops of trees, submerged houses with only the roofs showing, telegraph posts and so on. The sparrows had been just too wet and too miserable to get a move on.

In ordinary circumstances those sparrows undoubtedly would have fallen upon Boofie and beaten him up. They knew him all right. On numerous occasions they had feasted on the seed he had wastefully tossed from his cage as it hung on the side wall of the farmhouse in pre-flood days. They had often clung to the wires and sneaked seed that way. Boofie had always impressed them as being a snobbish, supercilious type of bird and many were the insults they had chirped at him.

Boofie, perched on a twig above their heads, eyed them uncertainly. They were not his kind, and, in any case, he always had been an unsociable bird. There had been one occasion when Mrs. Westwood had offered to care for a neighbour's canary while that neighbour was on holidays. Thinking that Boofie would like a companion, she had placed the visiting bird in his cage. As well as being a bit of company for Boofie, she considered it would save placing seed and water in two cages. The experiment was not a success. As Mr. Westwood had put it with a laugh, Boofie had started throwing punches at his guest as soon as it was introduced into his cage. Boofie had so hunted and harried that poor visitor, squawking harshly all the time, that it had to be returned to its own cage before it lost all its feathers. And the unrepentant Boofie had signalled his triumph by the greatest burst of melody the Westwoods had ever heard.

Now, although Boofie was an unsociable bird, he had a sudden yearning for a bit of company. Common adversity brought together strange acquaintances. These, of course, were not the first sparrows he had ever seen. They often used to hang around his cage for a free hand-out. He did not recognise this particular trio. All sparrows looked alike to him, even though the hens were plain and the cocks had black throats to proclaim their masculinity.

Five feet separated him from them and he made it easily. He alighted alongside a hen which looked sideways at him. Boofie sidled along until he was rubbing against the sparrow, which edged along in its turn, pressing against a cock bird. It gave an indignant chirp and pushed against the third of the trio, another hen, which stood fast. And there for a moment the four sat huddled—a case of birds not of a feather flocking together while a thin drizzle of rain fell on them.

Boofie was uncomfortable. In his cage he had been accustomed to take plenty of baths but at his own convenience. He objected to a bath being thrust upon him like this. So he ruffled his feathers and shook himself vigorously to the inconvenience of the sparrow next to him. It proved to be the last straw. The sparrow was fed up to the beak with everything and was ravenously hungry. With a squawk, it gave Boofie a hard peck, took to the air and flew swiftly towards the township, over a mile away. It was followed immediately by its two companions. The sparrows did not make the flight in one hop, however, but swooped down together on to the top cross-arm of a telegraph post sticking out of the water at a crazy angle on the river bank itself.

Boofie watched the exodus with surprise and indignation. At least those ill-mannered birds could have given him a hint of their intentions. Well, he would follow them. Launching himself from the branch, he went across the water in undulating flight. The telegraph post was a quarter of a mile away, but the canary had given no thought to the possibility that he might not be able to make it. His first long flight had been the fifty yards from the shed top to the tree, and this was about eight times that distance. His wings were not hardened to long hops and he found this out before he was half-way across the raging flood. His wings seemed to grow too heavy for his body and he appeared to have great difficulty in just flapping them.

As he laboured along he got lower and lower and he could do nothing to check the descent. And he was only six feet or so above the flood, and in imminent peril of dropping into it, when he sighted, coming down in the current, a floating tree that whirled and spun as the eddies played with it. Sheer good luck alone enabled him to reach and grab a protruding twig, and to this he hung for dear life. Happily for him, the uprooted tree was out of the full force of the river current, or he would have been submerged in no time and drowned. As it was, the tree spun around crazily and he was hard put to it to hang on. He was almost exhausted, too, by his unaccustomed flight.

Presently the tree swirled into a backwater along a breach in the embankment, and here it became wedged fast. But the force of the water rushing over it caused it to tremble violently, and Boofie was shaken about like a leaf in a gale. He was now several miles from his old home, with unflooded land seemingly as far away as ever.

And then he got the scare of his life. For some time he had been conscious of a loud noise, louder even than the flood waters, and then he saw, coming towards him, and low down in the sky, an enormous and most terrifying nightmare. It was making a horrific buzzing noise like ten million blowflies and was as big as a small house. As it obviously was flying it must be a bird, but what kind of a bird looked like that?

Poor Boofie crouched down on the trembling twig in terror as the helicopter thundered over him. It was an R.A.A.F. machine, carrying out fine rescue work among the stranded people, but how was a simple-minded canary to know that? Frantic, he hopped into the air and fled madly away, not caring in which direction he went or what became of him. Straight across the flooded river he travelled as if all the fiends in creation were on his yellow tail. He flew only a few feet above the waters because he just could not make height.

And then terror was added to terror as, glancing down, he became urgently aware of yet another terrifying thing. This was thudding its way up the river and making an awful din. When he first saw it, he baulked and managed to gain some height. Then he wheeled around and headed in the opposite direction. But all he could see was water and more water. His heart beating as if it would burst, he wheeled again and fluttered straight across the thing that was beating up the river.

And then his strength failed him completely. Little beak wide open, small heart pounding against his ribs, he fluttered and dropped straight down towards the deck of the army "Duck," landing upon the shoulder of Constable Jim Mead. For an instant he clung to the policeman's mud-stained jacket and then collapsed and fell on the deck itself.

"Stone the beetles!" exclaimed Mead. "Who's pelting me with dead canaries?"

"Huh?" asked a nearby soldier, Private Jack Thornton, who had been keeping a strict watch over the flooded countryside.

"Wonder where this little joker came from?" asked Mead as he stooped down and gently picked up the exhausted canary. Boofie was unhurt, but was completely done up. If the army Duck had not been in that precise spot when his strength had given out he would certainly have become another flood casualty.

Mead held the bird in his hand and stared at it.

"Well, I suppose he is just one of many," he remarked.

"By jove, I wonder how many dozens of pet birds and animals have been lost in this flood? Thank goodness his owner, whoever he was, had the decency to let him out and give him a chance."

"Not much chance for a canary in this show," said Thornton. "Wonder why his owner didn't take him with him? I'll bet there is a story behind this little coot's adventures."

"But what are we going to do with him?"

"Do with him? Why, nothing, I suppose. Just leave him alone, and when he has recovered let him go again."

"And the first cat will make a meal out of him."

"There are not too many cats in these parts," said Thornton drily. "They don't like the wet weather."

"I'll hang on to him," said Mead. "I'll shove him in a box or something and see if I can find a home for him when we get back to land. There's an old cardboard box kicking around here some place."

"Better tell the Old Man that we've taken an extra soldier on strength," grinned Thornton. "There is the matter of rations, you know."

The "old man" referred to was Warrant-Officer Harry Curlewis, who was in command of the Duck and at the moment was driving it. Mead said he wouldn't waste the time of the W.O. and, in any case, the question of rations did not enter into it, because none of them had rations, anyway.

By this time Boofie had got his wind back, and although he had not completely calmed down, he felt much better. Mead found the cardboard box and shoved him into it, securing the lid with a bit of string. As an after-thought he opened the box and put inside an old crust of bread. What Boofie really needed was a drink, but the constable did not think of this. With so much water around, it would be his last thought that anyone could possibly want to drink the dirty stuff.

Having stabbed a few airholes in the box with his knife—nearly transfixing Boofie as he did so—Mead placed the improvised cage in a corner out of the way and promptly forgot all about it. The crew of this Duck had much important work to do. Manned by experienced Army men, and with the constable as an important supercargo, the Duck had been working night and day rescuing stranded people from scattered dwellings. It was not the same Duck that had picked up Westwood. That vehicle was away patrolling another portion of the inundated countryside.

To say that Boofie did not like his new home would be to state it mildly. The box had once contained a pair of women's shoes—small shoes at that. In spite of the airholes, it was very stuffy, and the canary had to crouch on the bottom. Still, after a time, as he remained undisturbed, he began to perk up a bit, even to the extent of examining the crust of hard bread. He gave a few pecks at it, secured a beakful and swallowed it thoughtfully. It was not the class of food to which he had been accustomed, but it was eatable and better than nothing. Being hungry, he finished up making quite a meal out of it. But that bread was old and very dry, and if he had needed a drink before, he needed one much more after his feed.

And there was no water to be had. Most ironically, outside, the world around him was nothing but water, and, like the sparrows in the tree top earlier, he was now the Ancient Mariner—a real one—water, water, everywhere, and not a drop to drink.

But Boofie, thirsty as he was, was something of a philosopher in his own way, and quite used to being in captivity. There was nothing he could do to improve his position, so he withdrew into a corner of the boot box, tucked his head into his shoulder feathers, and went off in a doze.

CHAPTER FOUR

Canary at Large

BOOFIES awakening was not gentle. One moment he was in the canaries' dreamland, and the next he was jerked into wakefulness by the box being violently agitated. Constable Mead had picked it up and placed it under his arm.

The Duck was now splashing its way down the main street of the township between rows of inundated shops, and the constable thought he might be able to hand Boofie over to somebody to care for. There were still people living in the top portions of buildings and Mead felt certain that somebody would take the canary off his hands. The marooned people exchanged cheery greeting and humorous insults with the Duck crew as the vehicle lumbered by.

"What have you got in that box, copper?" shouted a young fellow hanging out of the second-storey window of a hotel. "If it's something to eat, chuck it up here."

"You'd have to be pretty hungry to tackle this," Mead shouted back. "What do you say to a cup of canary soup?"

"Wouldn't fill a hollow tooth!" roared the young fellow.

"You could leave the feathers on!" argued the constable.

"Not a chance. They'd tickle my insides out!" replied the young fellow with a shout of laughter.

"Well, how about taking the bird as a pet?"

"Keep him in case you feel lonely," roared the young fellow.

Mead offered Boofie to a number of other folk as the Duck proceeded down the street, but found no takers. Most of those he asked advised him to let the bird go free to take its own chances.

They said they had no food for themselves, let alone canary seed. Mead, who earlier had had notions of freeing Boofie, now grew obstinate. Somewhere, somehow, he would find a home for the bird. The Duck itself would not be returning to its base for some hours.

Applying an eye to one of the airholes he had punched in the box, he could just discern Boofie, who was sitting on the box bottom looking, and feeling, disconsolate. It was only a tiny atom of feathers and flesh, pondered the constable, yet it had as much right to live as anything or anyone. Perhaps it had been the cherished pet of some child, the beloved companion of some lonely old lady, or maybe just one of a flock of birds in a big aviary. It would now, of course, be quite impossible to find its real owner.

No matter how much he could and did sympathise with the lonely little bird, it never crossed the constable's mind to give it a drink. And Boofie needed one badly. He could not remember the last time he had quenched his thirst.

Once again he was stowed away in his box in a safe place, and the Duck's rescue work went on. It made many trips, sometimes taking people from flooded houses, sometimes transporting much-needed food and other supplies from the high ground to marooned folk whose premises could withstand the torrent, sometimes taking sick and injured to the hospital, which was out of flood reach. All this time the thirsty canary cowered in the old bootbox.

It was nightfall when the Duck crew was due to be relieved and Warrant-Officer Curlewis thankfully headed the vehicle to the flood-free ground. It followed the course of a submerged street, and as this street rose steeply the Duck emerged from the flood, water cascading from its six wheels in sheets and, becoming a road vehicle, drove off quickly to the School of Arts, where the crew could have a meal and a rest. Boofie, still in his box, of course accompanied them.

"I'm very much afraid you'll have to remain in that box indefinitely," said Mead, addressing Boofie through the cardboard lid. "I haven't got a cage and I'm hanged if I know where I'm likely to pick one up."

"Oh, let the thing go, Meady," said one of the crew members. "It's more trouble than it's worth. We can't be saddled with it. We've got plenty of work to do without looking after a silly bird. What do you say, boss?"

"Leave me out of it," replied Warrant-Officer Curlewis. "But I will say this: we can't have the bird with us on the Duck when we are working. It would be in the way. What Mead does with it otherwise is entirely his own affair."

"I'll think about it," said Mead. "In the meantime, I'll have a look how he is shaping."

Placing the box on the table and raising the lid slightly, he sneaked a hand inside. Boofie fluttered and squawked, scrambled on to the back of Mead's hand and, squeezing past it, hopped out on to the table. The constable made a grab at him, but he left the table and flew madly across the room—to crash into the opposite wall. The shock sent him to the floor, right into a pool of water that had leaked through a hole in the roof above. The feel of the water revived him and immediately he forgot everything else in his anxiety to quench his thirst. Instantly he was beaking up the precious fluid, making up for lost hours.

"Gosh," said Mead, who was watching him, "the poor little devil certainly had a thirst up. He's been all day without water. Now why didn't I think of that?"

"Because, as I told you before, we've all had too much on our minds to think about the needs of a dopey canary," said Private Fred Mansell, the soldier who had uttered the previous criticisms.

Instead of replying, Mead crept towards Boofie, intending to recapture him. Boofie had other ideas. The door and window of the room were both closed, so there was no chance of his escaping to the outside world.

Boofie saw Mead coming and left the floor with a rush of

wings. Up and up he went, to come to rest on the cross-beam up near the ceiling. The School of Arts was an old-fashioned place.

"How are you going to get him down from there?" asked Warrant-Officer Curlewis interestedly.

"Heave a boot up at him," suggested Private Mansell.

"If you do. I'll heave one at you," warned Mead. "We'll let him stop up there for the night. I'm too tired to go hunting canaries and the light isn't the best. I'll be glad when they get the electric light working again. An old hurricane lamp is not the best to see by. Anyway, the bird can stay up there out of harm's way and get a bit of shut-eye. We can all do with that. You know, if I could find a cage and get hold of some seed, I'd keep the little chap on the Duck as a mascot. What do you reckon, boss?"

"Not to be thought of," said Warrant-Officer Curlewis tersely.

"I'll tell you what I reckon," snorted Mansell. "I reckon you're plain nutty. You've been drinking too much floodwater. What use would a dashed canary be to us on that Duck? A dog might be handy, but a canary! For one thing, it would be in our way; for another we've got nothing to feed it on, and, finally, I don't like canaries. What do you other jokers say?"

Thus appealed to, the "other jokers" stated their views. Each one said he liked canaries in cages hanging on the wall at home, but they were unanimous in their opinion that Boofie would be an utter nuisance and completely in the way and out of place on a flood-rescue army amphibious vehicle.

"All right, all right," snorted Mead. "There is no need to make a song and dance out of it. I'm going to bed. I'll decide in the morning what I'll do with the bird. Nobody loves him."

"Nobody loves you while you act the goat over it, either," grunted Mansell. "Let the thing go and give it a break."

A scratch meal was quickly disposed of by the tired men and soon afterwards they were all stretched out on the floor, wrapped up in their army blankets. It had been a tough day and they were all glad to turn in. So was Boofie. Up above them on the beam, his head was already tucked into his shoulder feathers. In the distance the roaring of the floodwaters could still be heard. It acted as a grim lullaby as men and bird slept peacefully.

Boofie awoke next morning, as was his custom, as soon as it was light. From force of habit he gave himself a preening, running each long feather through his beak, investigating his breast-down and stretching each wing by pushing it out with a leg. Then he looked around the room. It was drab and uninteresting, but it might contain something to eat.

He took off from the cross-beam and flitted across to another ten feet away. Then the window attracted him and he dropped down on to the sill. Here he made a few pecks at some grains of sand, found them unpalatable, so flew down to the floor. All around him were gently moving heaps. From one of them came a sudden loud noise that sent the canary up into the air again; and from his safe perch on the cross-beam he peered down at the heap. Private Mansell had often been told by his mates that he snored like the roll of distant thunder, a charge that he always denied indignantly. Boofie, however, could have given evidence against him.

By now the canary was feeling very peckish, but there was nothing it could see to eat. It tried whistling a few bars, but gave that up. There was no fun singing on an empty stomach. Dropping down on to the table, he hopped around it, exploring everything. The tired Duck crew had not troubled to clear away after the evening meal, and there were plenty of breadcrumbs around. From these Boofie had his breakfast and then, hopping on to the edge of a saucer, peered suspiciously at the rather unattractive-looking liquid in it. He cautiously dipped his beak into it and had a sip. Why, it wasn't too bad at all! The sugary taste was, indeed, rather palatable. Thus Boofie had his first—and as it so happened, his last—drink of cold tea.

Fluttering back to his refuge on the high cross-beam, he indulged in another preening routine and felt on top of the world. So much so that, after a few preliminary chirps, he burst into full-throated song. And if there was one thing that Boofie could do really well, it was sing. He had a glorious range of melody and it rang out, clear and sweet, in the confined and stuffy room. He spared nothing of his repertoire, his liquid notes rising and falling and rising again into an intense crescendo that blanketed all other sounds; and for once the distant, sullen roar of the floods could not be heard.

Constable Mead stirred in his blankets and awakened. He was lying on his back and his eyes became riveted on the small yellow bird on the beam above him. He did not move lest he still that glorious voice. He could see Boofie's throat quivering violently with the energy he put into his melody.

"Not a bad sort of a whistler, that bird," said a voice at Mead's side.

"Not bad!" breathed the constable. "Man, he's a little trimmer!"

"Trimmer, my foot!" grunted Private Mansell from the other side of the room. "That noisy little coot woke me up. For two pins I'd sling a boot at him."

"You'll leave him alone, Mansell," exclaimed Mead. "What harm is he doing to you? Let him sing and be happy. There is precious little joy kicking around these parts just now."

"And, in any case, it's time you mugs were up and about the job," put in Warrant-Officer Curlewis.

Boofie, hearing the voices below, stopped his serenade and peered downwards with bright little black eyes. He felt safe enough where he was, but did not feel in duty bound to continue the free concert for these human beings, even though they had rescued him from the floods.

The Duck crew, with much complaining, forsook their blankets to face another long and tiring day. Boofie watched all their actions with keen interest. He always liked to know what was going on around him. In the hustle and bustle of washing, stowing away their sleeping gear and getting their breakfasts, the men forgot all about him, and it was only when they were on the point of leaving that Mead remembered.

"What are we going to do about that canary?" he asked the room at large.

"Please yourself, he's your bird," said Mansell. "Personally, I don't care if you put him in the next bird show or just wring his neck. Leave him where he is and let us get a move on. He'll be here when we get back tonight or some other time. Anyway, what the heck does it matter if he isn't?"

"I suppose if the door is kept closed and he stays up there, nothing will get him," said Mead. "Anyway, I'll have to take the risk."

"Oh, he'll be okay," said Warrant-Officer Curlewis. "Anyway, supposing he does get out? He'll find his way around all right. All the other birds have to look after themselves and get a living."

"Yes, bush birds, sparrows and starlings and so on," said the constable. "But he's a canary, hatched and reared in a cage like all canaries since the year dot. A fat chance he'd have of lasting more than ten minutes in the bush."

"Look," said Mansell impatiently, "we can't waste any more time here, Mead. You seem to forget that there is a flood on and that dozens of people are depending on us to get them out of trouble."

"Yes, I guess you're right," said Mead. "Righto, boys, let's get a wriggle on. Cheerio, old fellow; look after yourself. Be seeing you tonight if you're still here. I'll bring you some canary seed if I run across any."

With a cheery wave to Boofie he followed the rest of the Duck crew from the room, carefully closing the door behind him. Within seconds the men were aboard their craft and heading swiftly for the flooded township.

Boofie stayed aloft for some time after the men had gone and then dropped down to the table for another feed of breadcrumbs. It was poor old tucker to him, but the best available. A few grains of sugar provided a little variety and when he came upon an apple core he really went for it. Boofie loved apple cores. They had been a part of his staple diet at the Westwood home.

He was still pecking around the table when the door was opened stealthily. He did not hear it and the intruders, two boys, did not see him. These lads had no right in that room, which actually was a disused portion of the School of Arts, and they were up to no good. They had watched, from a distance, the departure of the Duck crew and now were exploring the men's quarters to see what they could acquire unlawfully in their light-fingered fashion.

Their first investigation was among the heaps of blankets which the Duck crew had stacked tidily along the walls. These yielded nothing. Then one of the lads, a sandy-haired young rip named Ben Barker, approached the table with vague thoughts of a free feed. And as he neared the table a streak of yellow shot from behind a milk jug, up past his head and came to rest upon a cross-beam.

"Hey, Whizzer, did you see that?" Barker yelled to his companion. "Look, a dashed canary!"

"Hey? Where?" exclaimed the other lad, glaring around.

"Up there on that beam. The thing was on the table here a minute ago."

"Gosh, yes, I see it." said Jack Perrett, who was affectionately known to his little playmates as "Whizzer." "Wonder how it got in here?"

"Dunno and don't care," said Barker. "Let out by somebody in the floods, or given to those Army blokes. Anyway, I'm gonna catch it. I could do with a canary."

"Me, too!"

"You lay off that canary, Whizzer! I saw it first and it's mine. I'll dong you if you try anything," said Barker.

"Where are you gonna get ten big men in a hurry to help you dong me, Fish-head?" sneered Perrett. "And, anyway, how are you gonna catch it? Shove some salt on its tail, huh?"

"You're a funny coot, Whiuer. If I was such a clever Alec as you I'd fly up there and hook it myself," retorted Barker with a touch of sarcasm. "I'll catch it by hunting it until it drops. Here goes for a start."

Saying which, young Mr. Barker, whose rather unattractive nickname was "Fish-head," took off his dilapidated cap and hurled it at Boofie. The cap was not heavy and did not reach the beam, so Fish-head looked around for something else to throw. There was a crust of bread on a plate on the table, so he shied this. It whizzed past Boofie's beak, startling him somewhat, but he stayed on his perch.

"This wants a bit of organising," declared Fish-head. "If we can hunt it down from that beam we can chase it around the room until it knocks up. Then we'll have it."

"We gotta decide first who gets it," insisted Whizzer Perrett. "I'm not gonna rush meself off me feet getting a bird for you, Fish-head."

It must be mentioned in passing that the derivation of the nicknames of the boys was one of those mysteries incapable of solution. Young Mr. Barker, though he was not handsome, had little or no resemblance to a fish, while young Mr. Perrett, rarely, if ever, whizzed.

"Let's catch the thing first, and then we can toss to decide who keeps it," suggested Fish-head, but Whizzer shook his head.

"That's out," he said flatly. "None of us won't own it. We'll sell it to old mother Gorton and halve the dough. Them things bring pretty good dough, specially in the breeding season. If it's a cock bird it is worth over a quid. Hens come a bit cheaper, but not much."

"Okay, I'm agreeable to that," said Fish-head. "I'd rather have the dough than the bird. Canaries are too big a nuisance to look after. Cyril Gorton told me that. Him and his old woman own a flock of them, and Cyril says they're always getting tummyaches and dying all over the joint. All right, then, that's settled. Now, as I said before, let's get organised. First of all, we've gotta get the thing off that beam, so chuck anything you can find at it."

Fish-head himself opened the barrage by again hurling his cap at Boofie. This time he put more beef into it and the flying headgear caught Boofie fair and square, sending him backwards off the beam. He took refuge in his wings and dashed madly across to the other beam. He had hardly settled on this when a military boot, hurled by Whiner Perrett, flashed past his beak and hit the ceiling with a loud bang. Boofie, in panic, took off again, and this time did a fast circuit of the room. The two boys kept up a loud shouting and hand-clapping, which terrified the bird, but did not induce him to fly any lower.

This annoyed Fish-head, and he began to throw things indiscriminately. First it was the companion boot of the one Whizzer had already thrown. This was followed by his cap again, then a rolled-up towel he had found folded on a heap of blankets. Whizzer caught the spirit of the affair and began to use the articles on the table.

It was quite hectic while it lasted. Poor Boofie flew round and round the room through a barrage of knives, forks, spoons, boots and towels. Then, in his utter madness, Whizzer seized the sugar bowl and sent it hurtling after the fleeing canary. It missed him by six feet and disintegrated against the wall. So did a cup. A saucer went swimming through the air and crashed through the window, reducing a large pane of glass to splinters.

"Hey, stone the nanny goats, break it down, Whizzer!" yelled Fish-head. "You'll wreck the joint. I think we'd better scram before somebody comes along and has us run in. They must have heard that broken glass half a mile away. Come on, let's beat it while our luck's in."

"What about the canary?"

"Hang the canary. I'm off!" said Fish-head, and, wrenching

open the door, scuttled through it without a backward glance.

Whizzer Perrett was close on his heels and he did not trouble to close the door behind him.

Boofie, with wildly-beating heart, was clinging to the top of the frame of a photograph depicting an ancient gentleman in a huge beard (a one-time president of the School of Arts). He stayed there for quite five minutes after the boys had gone. Then, realising that he was quite alone, he took heart again and began to interest himself in things. Cautiously he flew down on to the table and ate a few more breadcrumbs. Then he alighted on the floor and began to peck at the grains of sugar spilled from the broken sugar bowl. These were scattered all over the place, with quite a heap near the open door, and as he hopped about, Boofie passed over the threshold and out into the open world without immediately realising it.

At the side of the hall he came upon something he had not seen for days—a thistle. It was, indeed, the first time in his life that he had seen one actually growing. In next to no time his sharp little beak was eagerly chopping triangles out of the thistle leaves. It was a regular feast. He took time off to have a long drink from a pool of rain water nearby and then resumed his attack on the thistle. He disregarded a big slice of bread lying at the side of the pool.

Probably he would have stayed there until he had eaten the entire thistle had he not been interrupted. He heard the loud squawking of bird voices and next moment he was buffeted and pushed around as three starlings descended upon him, seemingly out of nowhere. The starlings were not interested in him. They wanted that slice of bread. The floods had made easy food scarce for these parasites of the bird world and they had to eat where and what they could. They had been passing overhead when their quick eyes had spotted the canary eating something. The starlings did not know what it was, but intended to find out, and as they dived to earth they saw the bread and went for it.

Such fighting and squabbling ensued! Poor bewildered Boofie was in grave danger of losing every feather he possessed as these large black birds pushed him and trampled on him in their eagerness to get at the piece of bread.

He succeeded in dragging himself to the outskirts of the melee and, spreading his wings, flew unsteadily to the limb of a peach tree nearby. Here he took stock of himself, the while casting fearful glances at the fighting starlings, who were kicking up an awful shindy over the bread. Then one wily old cock bird managed to stave off the challenge of the other two and, seizing the bread in his beak, whizzed into the air—making straight for Boofie's peach tree.

The startled canary did not wait for his arrival, but took off, flying blindly in the direction his beak happened to be pointing. He reached a thick privet hedge and dived into its interior. But the bread-carrying starling did not stop at the peach tree. It kept on going, the other two after it in full cry, squawking loudly and belligerently. They vanished over the tops of some distant trees and Boofie saw them no more.

The privet hedge in which he had taken refuge was a thick one, and he decided to stay there for a time. He felt safe. After a few minutes' rest he began automatically to preen himself. He had lost a few feathers during his adventures, but not enough to inconvenience him.

Presently he felt perky enough to want to sing. As an overture he commenced to trill softly to himself. Then he tried out a few louder bars. It sounded good. Next moment the surrounding countryside was receiving the full benefit of his glorious voice. He sang and sang as if his throat would burst, the feathers on it arching outwards as if growing on a small ball. He kept this up for several minutes and then lapsed into complete silence. A short nap seemed to be indicated. There was nothing else to do.

He was thinking about this when, within a few yards of him

there came a sudden burst of lovely canary melody. Boofie nearly
fell off his perch in astonishment and then craned his neck in all
directions. Though he never cared for company as a rule, he had
a sudden yearning to see another bird of his own species.

The song appeared to be coming from the privet hedge itself and
only a short distance away. Boofie decided to do a bit of detective
work. The hedge itself was too thick to fly through, so he began
to hop from twig to twig, making his way cautiously towards the
song. Then it stopped as suddenly as it began and Boofie looked a
little bewildered. He sang a few bars of inquiring song, but there
was no reaction. He hopped a few more feet and peered closely
through the leaves and twigs. There was no movement to proclaim
the presence of any other birds.

Having treated himself to another brief preen, Boofie settled
down on a twig for the delayed nap and then once again that
glorious canary song burst forth. This time Boofie hopped as fast
as he could towards the source and caught a glimpse of something
moving in a bush ahead of him. He sat still and watched. The song
had stopped now, but the canary kept his eye on what had moved.
Then he saw the creature. It was a bird, but it \vas nothing like a
canary. It was smaller and, in its way, much prettier than Boofie.

The little green bird with a circle of small white feathers around
each eye was clinging to a twig and twittering. Then Boofie saw a
similar bird. Probably its mate, because it twittered back. Apparently
neither of these birds had sung the canary song, but Boofie decided
to join them and inspect them at close quarters. Then he changed his
mind. They might treat him as those hooligan starlings had done.

Sitting on his own twig and watching the little green birds
hopping around in the hedge, Boofie got the surprise of his life.
One of the strange birds suddenly burst into glad canary song—a
replica of his own notes. Boofie put his head on one side and
stared. This was the strangest canary he had ever seen! Risking
everything, he hopped towards the little green songsters. They

saw him coming and beat a hasty retreat, chirping loudly as they went. Boofie flew after them, but he was no match in flight for the little silver-eyes, which swept away over the top of the peach tree and vanished from sight.

Boofie, perched in the peach tree, treated the whole matter philosophically. He did not have either the brains or the instinct to feel disappointed at losing such bright company, or indignant that a silver-eye should masquerade as a canary. Naturally, he was not aware that the silvereye was one of the most accomplished mimics in the bush, and could imitate the notes of almost any bird. The green songster early that morning had heard Boofie singing and had listened to an encore in the hedge. It had been easy for him to imitate the canary, and he had done so.

Boofie did not stay in the peach tree. It reminded him of the starlings. Returning to the haven of the privet hedge where there was nothing to disturb him, he took the nap he had promised himself before the advent of the silver-eyes.

CHAPTER FIVE

Bush Busybody

FROM his point of vantage in the air above the flooded country side, Nankeen Kestrel had a grandstand view of everything that went on below. Floods might bring ruin and devastation to all manner of living things, but they had not affected him to any material extent.

This was not Nankeen Kestrel's usual hunting ground. That was the paddocks, the farms and the crops over which he loved to skim and to hover in his search for grasshoppers, crickets and other insects, mice and other vermin. It was a good life, and useful, too. He was a friend of the farmers, because he helped to keep down pests of various kinds and never made a nuisance of himself in the chicken runs like his cousins, the collared sparrow hawk and the goshawk. Goshawk was a true chicken fancier, and, in consequence, was not loved by those human beings who kept poultry.

Kestrel, though driven from his usual hunting grounds by the floods, had nothing to complain about as regards food. The rising waters had driven all kinds of prey from their hiding places, and as these creatures thought only of saving themselves from death by drowning, they had scant time to think about death from any other cause —such as prowling hawks. Kestrel, therefore, by hanging around the edge of the waters, found many banquets ready for him as half-drowned mice, grasshoppers, crickets, spiders and many other delectable items sought safety on the unflooded ground.

Kestrel, whose habit was to dart down from the sky and capture his prey on the ground, uttering his excited chattering cry as he did so, was making his leisurely way over the treetops from the water when he noticed a slight disturbance down below. Two small birds seemed to be having a dispute about something. He paused in his flight and hovered over the disputants—a yellow bird about the size of a sparrow and of a type that was strange to him, and a larger bird with black and white plumage and a ridiculously long tail. The yellow bird was perched on the top of a fence post and the black and white one was flying around it in circles and chattering loudly.

Kestrel did not know the yellow bird, but he did recognise the black and white one. It was, of course, Willy Wagtail. There was no doubt about *that* bird. He was constitutionally incapable of keeping his beak out of other birds' affairs. He was troublesome, impudent and inquisitive and it was time that somebody took him down a peg. Kestrel felt like doing just that. He was well fed and inclined for a bit of sport. But before he interfered in the dispute it would be judicious to see what it was all about. So, ceasing his hovering, he flew on to the limb of a nearby gum tree, the better to watch the affair.

If Boofie had been at all wise in the ways of the bush creatures he would have known that Willy Wagtail would not do him the slightest harm. The long-tailed little villain with the black coat and white waistcoat did not have one tinge of viciousness in him, although, in the nesting season he could put up such a bold front that larger birds thought twice about molesting him. That, however, was merely Willy's courageous bluff. His little beak could not do much harm to anyone.

Boofie, sitting on the fence post, his wings half-raised and his beak open, was in fear of his life. The wagtail flew around him in circles, climbed into the air above him and dive-bombed him without pause, at the same time uttering his harsh challenging cry of "did-ja-did-ja-did-ja-did." Boofie had done nothing, and had not the faintest idea what it was all about. He wished heartily that he had stayed in the safety of the privet hedge.

Having had his nap, the canary, hunger again upon him, had remembered the thistle near the wall of the School of Arts. He had returned to it and was chopping fresh triangles from the leaves when he had been startled by something addressing him as "sweet pretty creature." He dimly recalled human beings talking to him in some such terms, but this was not a human voice. Whatever it was, he did not like it, so, deserting the thistle, he had headed back towards the privet hedge. But before he was half-way to that sanctuary he was knocked sideways in the air, and as he recovered himself, became aware of another bird flitting around him, the "sweet pretty creature" sentiments having given place to terms that were downright insulting!

The blow he had received was not severe, but it had the effect of forcing him to change direction, and instead of reaching the hedge, he found himself heading for the fence. He got to a post, and perched on the top, wondering what was coming next. He soon found out.

Willy Wagtail knew all the bush birds in his district and also most of the imported rubbish—the house sparrows, the starlings, the Indian turtle doves and the bulbuls, but he did not know any canaries. There were, of course, several so-called canaries among the bush birds, but their names had been bestowed by human beings who had little imagination.

First of all, there was the white-plumed honeyeater, a happy little green bird with a small tuft of white feathers behind his ears. He was, for some reason, called the Australian canary, in spite of the fact that he lived mostly on nectar taken from the flowers of the red gum, flower pollen, and, occasionally, insects. A lively little chap, he was never still, constantly flitting through the flowers and leaves and kicking up a great row as he did so. His loud, chattering song of "chick-o-wee" was nothing like a canary's melody. Apart from being miscalled the Australian canary, he also owned aliases of "Greenie," "linnet," "chickowee," "ringeye," and "ringneck."

Another alleged canary was the orange chat which dwelt mainly in the dry regions of the interior. This little bird was a sociable soul and belonged in a flock. He never got around on his own. Unimaginative humans had called him the "saltbush canary," and while they were about it had also pinned on him the label of "yellow tintac." His song was very mediocre, consisting of a rather metallic "ting-ting-ting-ting." He, too, favoured insects at meal time.

Third of the so-called canaries was the white-throated warbler. He masqueraded under several names—"bush canary," "native canary," "fly-eater," and "bush warbler," and was a swagman among the birds. His usual home was in the far north, but in the springtime he "humped his bluey" southwards to N.S.W. and Victoria. Whitethroat did possess a very sweet song, but nothing like a genuine canary. His lunch basket, too, was packed with insects and grubs.

The fourth Australian "canary" was the mangrove warbler, who rarely strayed further afield than southeastern Queensland. In addition to being nicknamed the Queensland canary, some folk called him the "singing fly-eater." He dwelt among the mangroves and scrub, and existed upon insects of all kinds. As for his voice, it was really beautiful—in fact, some folk regarded it as the sweetest song of all the warblers. But he was not a canary.

All these alleged canaries lived on insects, whereas Boofie and his family preferred seed. Insects would have given them a pain under the breast feathers.

Of course, Willy Wagtail knew all about these birds. He knew all about everything. In any case, he had nothing to preen his own feathers about as far as names were concerned. Established custom had labelled him Willy Wagtail, but certain folk knew him as "black and white fantail," "shepherd's companion," "morning bird" and "frog bird." Why the latter, when he had no use at all for frogs, was not clear.

There was, however, one thing on which he could pride himself if he cared. He was the only bird in the whole of the Australian bush who had what might be termed a family name. He was "Willy Wagtail." One of his relations, the brown flycatcher, was known as "Jacky Winter," but "Winter" was a poor old surname. Willy was a wagtail, but Jacky was not a "winter." Then there was "Micky Miner" the soldier bird, who certainly was not a toiler in the bowels of the earth. Jacky Winter, however, was as friendly a bird as cousin Willy, and had the same habit of swaying his big tail from side to side. His sweet song, however, was spoiled at times by his yelling out, "Peter, peter, peter." Not that he knew anyone named Peter, but because Nature had wished that call on to him. And, like so many of his feathered friends and relations, he had almost as many aliases as a burglar —"Peter-peter," "postboy," "post-sitter," "white-tail," "stump-bird" and, for goodness' sake, "spinks"!

But Willy Wagtail at the moment had no interest in the names and habits of other bush birds. His attention was concentrated upon this strange yellow bird and he intended to beat it up just because it was strange. It was bad enough having to put up with the ordinary birds in the district without strangers like this invading the place. Let him go back to where he came from, and permit the established birds to live their lives in peace and in their own territory. There was too much of this business of migrants trampling upon the vested interests of the native inhabitants.

And as he proceeded to make Boofie's life miserable, Willy Wagtail did not for a moment pause to consider what an inconsistent hypocrite he was. For Willy Wagtail, when he felt like it—and that was from dawn until dusk—would attempt to beat up any native resident bird he saw, from a diminutive emu wren to a mighty wedgetailed eagle. He was courageous beyond belief, and a plain, unvarnished nuisance, and yet, among human beings, was one of the most popular and lovable little birds in the bush. Nobody could help but feel affection for Willy Wagtail.

Boofie, not being a gullible human being, could not see one thing to love about the long-tailed little wretch who darted at him and past him with snapping beak. Boofie did a bit of snapping back, and had Willy been another canary, Boofie promptly would have sailed into him, for the canary was no coward; but the wagtail was a strange-looking bird and might possess many unknown and dangerous qualities. So Boofie decided to play it safe.

Willy could see that he had the canary bluffed, and was greatly pleased. He alighted on the fence a few feet away and eyed Boofie speculatively. Strange-looking object—like a sparrow, but different. A sparrow would not have put up with the ragging he had dished out to Boofie. Willy swayed from side to side, his long tail waving like a signal flag, and then he edged along the rail a little closer, at the same time chattering loudly. Boofie watched his approach with apprehension, raised his wings and chirped loudly. Willy accepted the challenge and darted at him—at exactly the same moment that Boofie lost his head and darted at Willy. They met chest-on, and Willy gave back a little in sheer astonishment. Then, before he realised what was going on, he found himself being pushed earthwards with Boofie on top of him. Willy gave an extra loud screech that did him no good at all. Boofie, fed up to the bill with being pushed around, began to peck and scratch at the wagtail, and Boofie's beak was really sharp. Willy felt several feathers detach themselves from his body, and when the canary peeked him right in the eye he felt it was time to throw the sponge in. He had caught a Tartar.

It was not lack of courage that caused Willy to withdraw from the engagement. The wind had been taken completely out of his sails. Leaving Boofie on the ground, he streaked off as fast as he could fly, and did not stop until he reached the highest twig of the highest gum tree in the neighbourhood. Here he took stock of himself and tossed up whether he should return to the attack. He had his mind made up for him when he heard a loud chattering call in his ear. He turned sideways and looked straight into the eyes of Nankeen Kestrel. In ordinary circumstances, Willy would have chattered back his defiance, but after the encounter with the strange yellow bird his nerve had been shaken.

So, handing over complete occupancy of the tree to the hawk, Willy streaked off.

Peering downwards, Nankeen Kestrel saw the canary fly up on to the top of the post again and examine its feathers. This done, the yellow bird flew to the next post, where it paused for a few moments. Then it took off again and flitted down the fence. Kestrel felt half-inclined to follow it, but changed his mind and, leaving the gum tree, flew leisurely towards the floods and the easy banquet he hoped to obtain.

CHAPTER SIX

Boofie Goes Bush

BOOFIE continued his post-hopping until he came to the point where the fence continued at right-angles. He sat on the top of the corner-post for a time and looked around him. In front was a patch of tea-tree scrub on a vacant allotment. To the right the fence continued down the side of a lane that led to water, while to the left were houses. The only vestige of life was a horse grazing near the scrub on the vacant land. Of human beings there was no sign. Remembering the privet hedge, he decided to make for the scrub, and did so, flitting across the intervening space and giving the horse a wide berth.

He perched for a moment on a tea-tree twig and then flitted through the scrub, to find himself among tall gum trees. This was the beginning of the bush proper. As he progressed, he heard the chirps and twitterings of birds and now and then caught glimpses of various feathered creatures fluttering among the leaves and branches; but as they did not interfere with him, he felt no fear. What he did feel, however, was hunger. He had not eaten since the small snack off the thistle. What he needed was a good tuck-in of canary seed, but there was none of that to be had.

Perching on a gum twig, he had a good look around. It was now mid-afternoon, and though the trees and bushes still glistened from the long rains and the grass and undergrowth was sodden, the sun had made its appearance again, and was shining from an almost cloudless sky. How long this pleasant state of affairs would continue was a matter of conjecture, but, rain, hail or sun, the bush creatures had their busy lives to live and their main business was the never-ending search for food.

Boofie had his gum tree to himself. He was perched on a twig jutting from a branch at least fifteen feet from the ground, the branch joining the trunk about a dozen feet from where he sat.

Suddenly his attention was caught by a pair of small blackish-brown birds who had appeared as if from nowhere and were squabbling at the foot of the tree. These newcomers, who were calling to each other in rather sharp voices, had long slender bills curved downwards, and long, curved, sharp claws. Ceasing their argument, they began to hop around among the leaves and dead twigs on the ground, picking at the rotten bark and peering into crevices in the tree trunk itself. As Boofie watched they began to run up the trunk, but not in a straight line. They went round and round it in a spiral, gaining height all the time, pausing now and then to examine holes in the bark. They were brown tree-creepers, and they were going about the serious business of meal-getting. Spiders and insects lurking in crevices in the bark had little chance of escaping their keen eyes and eager beaks.

And as they worked up the tree trunk, Boofie's attention was again distracted, this time by chatterings from a tree nearby. He looked and saw a little bird with a short tail, long, pointed wings, sharp straight beak and long, strong claws. It was brown and white and had orange markings on the wings. It, too, was exploring the other tree for insects, but whereas the tree-creeper was making up the trunk, this bird was going downwards —head-first and without any trouble. The bird was an orange-winged sittella or nuthatch. Nor was it alone, for, heading down the trunk behind it, Boofie saw half a dozen similar birds.

The hunting could not have been profitable, because, before it had gone very far, the sittella, chattering loudly, flew across into Boofie's tree. It was followed by all its friends and relations, the whole flock alighting in the top of the tree. By almost dislocating his neck, Boofie saw them starting off in single file down the trunk, headfirst, of course. The leader went straight down the tree, but some of his friends ran along branches, peering and peeking into holes and cracks. And a fine noise they made about it, too.

In the meantime, the two brown tree-creepers were still ascending the trunk, spiralling upwards. And they reached the point where the branch on which Boofie was perched joined the trunk, at exactly the same moment as the descending sittellas. The tree-creepers looked at the sittellas and the sittellas looked at the tree-creepers. Had they been woodpeckers they would probably have assaulted each other and waged a battle in the tree-tops, but they were not. There were no such things as woodpeckers in the Australian bush, though both sittellas and tree-creepers had been labelled such by ignorant human beings.

The two species of birds paused when they met, eyed each other narrowly-—and then they all flew away, the tree-creepers to a nearby tree and the whole flock of sittellas through the bush and out of sight. They were wise birds. The tree-creepers realised that if the sittellas had been prospecting the top of the gum tree there would be no insects left up there for the tree-creepers, while the sittellas on their part knew that it would be useless continuing down the tree, the trunk of which had already been given a thorough going-over by a pair of hungry tree-creepers.

Before Boofie really had time to give a thought to the matter his ears were assailed by a loud chattering noise and into his tree swept a squad of rather large blue-grey birds with black and white head markings and yellow patches around the eyes. They all landed on a branch below the canary, and immediately began to fight and squabble among themselves. Such a squawking and pecking went on that Boofie took fright and whizzed up on to a higher branch, secreting himself in a bunch of gum leaves from where he could see without, he hoped, being seen.

The birds down below were among the noisiest and most

quarrelsome and most inquisitive in the Australian bush; in fact, they were much worse than Willy Wagtail, if that were possible. In the bush they attended to everyone's business but their own. So did Willy Wagtail, but Willy, with all his reputation as a busybody, was a friendly soul and never quarrelsome. These birds, Noisy Miners, were bold without being friendly. They, too, had a string of nicknames, mostly uncomplimentary, such as "garrulous honeyeater," "black-headed miner," "snake-bird," "cherry-eater," "soldier bird," "Micky Miner," and "black-headed flower-sucker."

For human beings they had absolutely no time whatever. The mere appearance of a human in their neighbourhood was sufficient to cause a loud clamour of disapproval. And their own popularity among other birds was practically nil. Restless, noisy and overbearing, the miners lived on insects, fruit, berries and flower pollen.

But Noisy Miner was not all bad. If there was a thing he hated more than a human being, it was a snake, the sight of one causing him and his friends to set up such a din that the bush for miles around was disturbed. Many a bird had reason to thank the miners for this service, and so did plenty of human beings. And many birds had deeper reason to be thankful to the miners for their dislike of human beings. For the miners, being such expert sentries, spotted humans prowling with their guns and traps and catapults, and warned birds far and wide by their raucous protests. Micky Miner was, indeed, the bane of the human hunter's existence.

It was well for Boofie that the miners were unaware of his presence in the leaves above them, or it would have been the end of him. They were not butcher birds in the ordinary sense—they had no interest in other birds as food; but their inborn inability to mind their own business would have sent them crowding around and ganging up on this strange yellow newcomer, and the undoubted end of their examination would have been a demise in the canary world. They were none too gentle in their ways.

Presently the whole flock of rowdy larrikins took off and flew away across the bush to where a solitary banksia tree grew upon the edge of a waterhole. Here they settled and resumed their brawl. One bad-tempered bird, disputing his perching place with another, was knocked spinning, and before he could recover himself had hit the surface of the brimming waterhole. Undaunted, he flew back to the tree, but his mishap had started something. One of his mates immediately flew down to the water and, on reaching the surface, lifted his wings high and plunged his body into it. He was careful not to wet those wings, otherwise he might not have been able to get back to dry land, or, rather, dry tree. The rest of the flock, squawking loudly, proceeded to play follow-the-leader, diving to the water, wetting their bodies and returning to the tree. It was great fun while it lasted and they seemed to enjoy it, which was surprising. Micky Miner was a bird who never seemed to get any fun out of life.

The miners were still at it when Boofie decided to move on—in a direction opposite to that where the birds were bathing.

He flitted through the trees without adventure until he reached a small, well-grassed clearing studded with low scrubby bushes and, observing a shallow puddle-hole, dropped down to have a drink. The water was muddy, but it was a case of take it or leave it. Boofie took it. He was still poking around the mudhole when he was joined by a dozen or so little birds which, taking no notice of him, began to drink thirstily. They were double-bar or banded finches, and they lived among the scrubby bushes and grasslands where they existed well on berries and the seeds of a variety of plants.

Boofie looked anxiously at the newcomers, expecting a hostile move, but when the little birds made no attempt to assault him, he ventured to chirp a greeting. One little finch, who, like his mates, had a white face, a brown speckled body, a light waistcoat, a black bar across his throat and another across his chest, chirped back. It was all peaceful and friendly-like.

Having had their drinks, the finches flew off in a flock into the scrub and Boofie followed them. They did not remain long among the bushes, however. Hungry, like all birds, they dropped down into the grass and began to fill up on seeds. Boofie did likewise, and by noting where the double-bars fed, and copying them, he managed to do quite well for himself. It was his first feed of seeds since his cage days. The finches did not object to his presence, so Boofie stayed on with them, and when night fell he went to roost with them among the thick bushes.

It seemed like years since the floods had disrupted his life, but it was only a couple of days. A great deal, however, had happened to Boofie in that period.

Next morning he awakened at dawn and the sun was shining brightly as he and the double-bars had breakfast. He stayed with them all that day and again camped with them that night. They did not move far from the security of the thick scrub, and in their friendly and innocent company Boofie found peace and contentment.

CHAPTER SEVEN
The Black Star Gang

THE floods were a gift from the gods to Ben "Fishhead" Barker, Jack "Whizzer" Perrett and the handful of other young larrikins who comprised the "Black Star Gang." They all lived on the high ground, and as their school was under many feet of water and mud, they stayed at home and made miserable the lives of their families.

In a community so stricken by hardship that the hearts of the people almost failed them when they thought of the tremendous rebuilding days ahead, there was plenty of work to do for willing and able hands. So much so, that towns in many parts of the State had sent eager contingents of men and material to help in the long task of reconstruction.

All this, of course, had no interest for the Black Star Gang. Nobody was going to make them work. Their homes had not been touched by the floods, so why should they worry? In addition to that, no rain had fallen for a week and already the water was going down. The days again were hot and sunny and the countryside away from the inundated areas was dry and pleasant—just the kind of weather to go shooting, trapping or camping out.

So Fish-head Barker and Whizzer Perrett had summoned a meeting of the gang to make their plans. The gang met in the tool shed at the rear of the Barker residence, and Fish-head was chairman. Had formal minutes been kept of the proceedings the record would have shown that those present included Francis

Algernon Montgomery Wilberforce Webb, known, owing to the shortness of life, as "Spider"; Henry John George O'Neill, more popularly called "Skinny"; Alexander Malcolm Ian MacTavish, strangely nicknamed "Mad Dog"; and an angel-faced youngster, Cyril Fitzherbert Gorton, whose most inappropriate alias was "Butch." Cyril looked like a violet growing out of a bed of prickly-pear when he foregathered with that mob. He lived with his widowed mother, who lavished upon him all the care and affection that a fond mother could bestow upon an only child.

Cyril's ticket of admission to the Black Star Gang consisted of his ability to supply almost anything the mob required. Mrs. Gorton was most extravagant where Cyril was concerned. He had but to ask and she gave freely. Cyril, therefore, was welcome among the Black Star gangsters and was treated, if not with respect, at least with tolerance. He was never beaten up, or otherwise ill-treated. It was bad luck for him that there were no other boys of his gentle disposition in that neighbourhood. If he wanted playmates of his own age he had to string along with the Black Star Gang—like a butterfly consorting with a squad of trapdoor spiders.

At their meetings, each member of the gang wore pinned to his dirty shirt—in the case of Cyril to his nice clean coat—a rough star cut out of tin and daubed with black paint. The gang also had a plentiful supply of black cardboard stars, and on Empire Night, New Year's Eve and similar festive occasions when they placed double-bungers and other species of fireworks in the letter boxes of clergymen and nervous old ladies—and shattered both the box and the peace of the neighbourhood—it was their custom to leave a black star on the ruins as a kind of visiting card.

Fish-head Barker stared at his henchmen who sat around him in a semi-circle on old boxes and told them all to keep their mouths shut until he had finished making an announcement. They kept their mouths shut as ordered.

"It's about time we did something exciting, you jokers," he

commenced. "We haven't had a chance for any fun since the floods started. Yes, I know we got a bit of amusement out of slinging rocks through windows when nobody was looking and the mugs all thought the rushing water did it, but that was kid stuff. We've got to do something to stop ourselves going blue-mouldy."

"Too right," said Mad-dog MacTavish. "Let's go and stick a match to the rotten school."

"A dashed bright lurk," said Fish-head. "But seeing that it's under about thirty feet of water, how do you propose to go about it, you stupid-looking nitwit?"

"Aw, I forgot that," admitted Mad-dog.

"Do you think we could hire a boat somewhere and go out taking food to people stranded in the floods, Benjamin?" asked Cyril, who rarely referred to any of the gang by their nicknames. "That would be a jolly fine thing to do, I think."

"Are you trying to be funny, Butch?" snorted Fishhead, while the rest of the gang directed incredulous glances at Cyril. "If you are, you're liable to stop a bunch of fives right on your little snout."

"By jove, Benjamin, I do not think that is humorous," protested Cyril. "Mother says that lots of people still need assistance and that many will never recover from their losses."

"Well, you go home and tell your old woman to go and help them. We've got other fish to fry," said Fish-head—an unfortunate remark, because it permitted Spider Webb to indulge in a coarse and ribald comment.

"I'll fry *your* flaming head, Spider, if you don't stop trying to be funny," exclaiming young Mr. Barker. "Listen, what's wrong with all you jokers today? Can't you do something instead of crack silly jokes? All right, then. I'm not gonna make a speech. I'm gonna issue orders and you mugs have got to get cracking without any backchat, see? We're all gonna go trapping birds in the bush and we're gonna camp out for the night, maybe two nights. All those against, kindly raise the right hand and I'll knock your blocks off!"

"Whacko!" exclaimed Skinny O'Neill. "That sounds hot dog if we can work it."

"And why shouldn't we be able to work it?" demanded the chairman.

"My old man might crack down on me," said Skinny morosely.

"And I'm very much afraid that my dear mother would never permit me to stay out all night in a tent," said Cyril, shaking his head. "She gets so lonely, you know."

"Any of you other mugs got any objections to make?" demanded Fish-head. "Apparently my idea is crook. Obviously none of you jokers want to trap birds and camp out for the night."

"Oh, I guess we all want to, Fish-head, but if our parents won't let us we can't," said Whizzer Perrett.

"Anyway, where would we get a tent from?"

"That's all fixed. We'll use Mad-dog's," said Fish-head. "We've used it before. That'll be jake, eh, Maddog?"

"I suppose so," responded young Mr. MacTavish. "But it wouldn't have hurt you to ask me first, Fishhead."

"Aw, cut out the palaver, you Scotch mug," said young Mr. Barker discourteously.

"I'm an Australian," said Mad-dog indignantly. "So is my old man. It was my grandfather who was a Geordie."

"All right—you Australian mug, if that suits you better," said Fish-head impatiently. "Anyway, all you blokes see if you can fix it to go trapping on Saturday and camp out that night. It should be okay. I'll bet your families will be glad to get rid of you."

"Okay, Fish-head," chorused the gang, with the exception of Cyril, who remarked, "My mother would never be glad to get rid of me. However, I would love very much to camp out with my friends, and I may be able to arrange it with mother. But I do not care for trapping birds. I do not think that the beautiful wild bush birds should spend their lives in cages. It is not right."

"Look who's talking," said Spider Webb. "That comes lovely from you, seeing that you and your old woman have got about thousand canaries. They're birds, aren't they?"

"Me and Fish-head almost caught a canary the other day and were going to sell it to your old woman," put in Whizzer Perrett.

"Canaries are different. They have been born and reared in cages ever since the 16th century," said Cyril. "And I haven't got a thousand, either. My mother and I have about twenty birds. And you all really must refrain from referring to her as the old woman. I do not not like it."

"Twenty-four canaries, eh?" asked Fish-head. "Well, if you camp out they can keep the old girl company. And if we can catch a swag of redheads, diamond sparrows or double-bars, you can set up your own aviary."

"I don't want to set up an aviary of bush birds, and I really must again ask you not to refer to my dear mother as the old girl or the old woman," cried Cyril protestingly.

"Okay, okay, keep your hair on, Butch," said Fishhead with a chuckle.

"And I suppose," put in Spider Webb, "that, seeing none of you clever dicks have any bird traps, you'll want to borrow mine?"

"Naturally," said Fish-head. "How did you guess?"

"So we are gonna use Mad-dog's tent and my traps. What are you other jokers going to bring along, apart from your sweet selves? I suppose you'll put the hooks into Butch to provide all the eats? The poor dill generally falls for that racket."

"I'm not a dill . . ." began Cyril indignantly.

"Of course, you're not, Cirry," protested Fish-head. "As for you, Spider, you know quite well that we wouldn't expect Butch to cater for the mob. We'll be quite fair in this. You provide the traps and Mad-dog will bring the tent. That will let you two out of bringing any eats. Cyril can bring along enough tucker to cover himself and you two, and the rest of us will bring our own. Of course, we will all take our own blankets. Pyjamas are out, naturally. We can sleep in our togs."

"Of course," nodded the gang in unison—except Cyril.

"Er, I don't know, Benjamin—" he began, but Fishhead patted him kindly on the back. "Sure, Butch, that's okay. You can wear your nice frilly pyjamas if you want to, can't he, gang?"

"Oh, sure," chorused the gang.

"Thanks, chaps, but I was really going to talk about all that food you want me to bring. There are floods on, you know, and . . ." began the lad.

"Say no more about it," said Fish-head generously. "No need to thank us. We know you like doing good turns for the gang, don't we, mob?"

"Too right! Good old Butch!" shouted the gang heartily.

"Gee, thanks, chaps. I'm really grateful and I shall do my best," said Cyril, his eyes misty. Even if he felt some little doubt about the whole thing, he could not possibly let down these marvellous pals of his. How kind and generous they were!

"Now, listen to me, you mugs," said Fish-head before the conference adjourned, "keep this under your hats and don't spread it around. We don't want any funny business with the rest of the blokes in this town. Remember once before when some of us camped out and that Dooley crowd got to know about it and pulled down the tent on us while we were all asleep. We don't want any of that this time."

Having extracted a promise from each of his adherents that mouths would be kept tightly closed, Fish-head closed the meeting and they all went home, it having been arranged that they would meet again next morning to make final plans, based on the number that would be permitted to camp out.

There was great jubilation at this meeting when it was revealed that parental permission had been unanimous. It would appear

that the Barker, Perrett, O'Neill, Webb and MacTavish families
were not averse to getting rid of their little darlings for a whole day
or night. Indeed, Barker senior had stated flatly that he would not
care a continental red cent if his son and heir did not come home
for a month. Even gentle Mrs. Gorton had kindly consented to
her little boy going along. The whole point was that she was not
acquainted personally with any of the Black Star Gang. Cyril,
for obvious reasons, had never invited any of them to his home,
but his reports to his mother had painted them all as his fellow
angels. The gang, knowing their own limitations, and also not
desiring to precipitate anything that might bring about the loss
of Cyril's bountiful and generous friendship, always studiously
avoided the Gorton mansion. If any of them met Mrs. Gorton
in the street they addressed her as respectfully as they knew how.
Added to all that was the fact that Mrs. Gorton herself had no
interest in any human being outside Cyril and did not want to
be friends with his friends.

The great Saturday dawned, warm and sunny. The gang
assembled at the Barker shed to take stock of their possessions.
Cyril came along trundling a billy cart which was packed with
provisions of all kinds, a fact that made the gang lick its collective
lips and cause Mad-dog MacTavish to suggest that they should,
there and then, fall to work upon the provisions and have an
enormous feed. This proposal was negatived by the rest of the
Black Stars. Cyril said he had had a difficult last-minute job getting
away from his mother, but at length she had allowed him to
depart, and there he was.

"And extremely nice, too, Butch!" commented Fishhead.

Off they started, young Mr. MacTavish staggering under the
weight of the tent, which nobody offered to assist him to carry;
Spider Webb bearing two large bird traps, with a redhead in one
and a double-bar in the other; Cyril Gorton pushing his billy
cart of provisions, blankets and other odds and ends, and the rest

wearing haversacks and carrying blankets, billy cans, a frying pan and other necessary camping equipment.

They had not gone very far before Mad-dog announced that he was sick of carrying the heavy tent. He dumped it on top of Cyril's billy cart. Cyril did not protest—he just grunted and pushed harder. Spider Webb then placed his bird traps on top of the tent, but one of them fell off, endangering the life of the double-bar "caller," so he decided to carry them.

"You blokes lay off Butch and do your own carrying," said Fish-head sternly. "He's got enough to handle now without you loading his cart up. However, my airgun won't take up much space, so I'll let Cirry have that on his load."

Saying which, young Mr. Barker rammed the stock of the gun down the side of the cart, leaving the muzzle pointing skywards like a signal mast. Cyril made no complaint.

Reaching the bush, the gang decided to erect the tent in a clearing not far from a waterhole. For once everyone did a bit, and the tent was soon up and the gear stowed inside.

"Now, before we go any further, we've got to decide on sentries," said Fish-head. "We can't all go away at once. Somebody might come along and pinch our stuff. Well, seeing that Butch doesn't like trapping—" he paused suggestively and Cyril fell for it.

"I'll be only too delighted to stay here and guard the things while you chaps do your trapping," he said warmly. "I do not object in the least—in fact, I am grateful for your trust in me."

"Good old Butch!" cried Fish-head, slapping him on the back and almost precipitating him into the waterhole. "You're elected."

"Whacko! Good old Cyril!" endorsed the rest of the gang. "Our best old cobber!"

"Gee, thanks, chaps!" said Cyril, his heart expanding under their praise. "Thanks for your trust in me. It will not be misplaced, on that you may rest assured."

"We know that, Cirry, old horse!" said Whizzer Perrett.

Skinny O'Neill, who knew the surrounding bush well, or said he did, voiced the opinion that the best place for trapping was another clearing about half a mile away. It was, he alleged, crowded out with fire-tailed finches, double-bars, plumheads, diamond sparrows, zebra finches, honeyeaters and other birds. To the sarcastic comment of Mad-dog MacTavish that, if there were so many birds there they must get in each other's way, Skinny replied coldly that seeing was believing. So, signalling to Spider Webb to bring along his traps, he marched away through the scrub. Spider, bearing the traps, followed him, the rest of the gang bringing up the rear in Indian file.

Left to his own devices, Cyril set about arranging and rearranging the amenities of the camp. First of all, he carefully unloaded his billy cart, bringing to light cakes, biscuits, tins of preserved fruit, bread, butter, sweets, bacon, eggs, a tea pot, tin of sugar, bottle of milk, cup and saucer, cutlery, a small table cloth and two serviettes. All these he stowed away neatly in the tent and then arranged the blankets of the other lads, allotting them all sleeping places. It appeared to him that they would all be jammed in like sardines in a tin, but that would not matter for one night. It would be jolly, actually!

Next he prepared to make a fire. Casting around, he discovered a shallow hole in the ground and he decided to make this the camp fireplace. Having gathered some sticks and dried grass, he soon had a fire going, and on this he resolved to boil a billy. But what about water? Nobody had thought about clean water! He eyed the surface of the nearby mudhole in grave doubt. It was coffee-coloured after the rains, but he had often heard that any water was wholesome if it were boiled. Anyway, it would be quite an adventure, roughing it like this in the great Australian bush. The old explorers and pioneers who had opened up the vast spaces for settlement had had to exist on muddy water. So Cyril put on the fire a can filled with muddy water. This, he told himself, was, indeed, the life!

CHAPTER EIGHT

Trapped!

CYRIL was still fussing around the fire when the birdtrappers returned two hours later. He had boiled away at least three billies of water and had grown a little tired of keeping the fire going. It was hard work collecting sticks all the time.

Luck had been dead out for the trappers, as Fish-head Barker proclaimed loudly as he came in sight of the tent. He attributed the whole lack of success to Skinny O'Neill. Hadn't that liar told the world that the bush was completely packed with all types of birds just waiting to be trapped? Yes, he had. Was the bush crammed with birds all queuing up ready to step into the traps? No, it dashed-well wasn't. Hadn't they spent hours and hours searching for birds to trap? Too right they had. Did they find any? No, by gosh they didn't!

"Oh, go boil your fishy head, Fish-head!" howled Skinny, stung to a retort. "You're such a clever know-all yourself, ain't you? You couldn't find any birds, so stop taking it out on me."

"Did I rush around the countryside telling everyone that the bush was packed tight with them?"

"Listen, Fish-head, if you keep harping on that, I'll drop you, big and ugly as you are!" howled Skinny O'Neill.

"You and who else?" snorted Fish-head. "I'll have you on, any time you feel like it, you nitwit."

He squared up to Skinny in a fighting attitude and invited him to step forward and have his head knocked off. Cyril Gorton was horrified.

"Oh, please, chaps, don't go and spoil things by fighting," he begged. "Calm down and have your dinner and you will both feel much better. You may have better luck trapping this afternoon. Come on, chaps, do shake hands."

"Okay, but that Skinny O'Neill coot had better keep his big gob shut about dropping me," said Fish-head with a surly grunt.

"And that fish-headed mug had better ease off about me being responsible for us not catching any birds," said Skinny sulkily.

"Oh, shut up the two of you and let us have a feed," said Spider Webb. "Come on, Mad-dog. Leave these two jokers to it."

"There is something I want to mention, chaps," said Cyril, now that an uneasy peace had been established. "We did not bring any drinking water and I'm afraid that that stuff in the waterhole is scarcely palatable. What shall we do? I've boiled up some, but it looks a little murky to me."

"Aw, just chuck a handful of tea into the billy can and stew it up. Nobody will notice the difference," said Fish-head. "It won't kill us."

"Well, if you say so," said Cyril doubtfully. "And what are we going to eat for lunch?"

"That depends on what you have brought along, Butch," said Mad-dog MacTavish.

"I have all sorts of nice things. Have a look for yourselves," invited Cyril. The gang needed no second invitation and by the comments expressed, each of them appeared to be intensely gratified by the extent of Cyril's larder. Fish-head suggested that they have a light meal and save up the good things until night, when they could turn on a banquet. He said he had brought along a bag of tomatoes and raw onions and he intended to make a light lunch of raw onion and tomato sandwiches—a meal in which Cyril was quite welcome to share. Cyril, shuddering slightly, said that he would open a tin of sardines and use them for his sandwiches.

As for drink, he did not feel like tea, so would content himself with a bottle of lemonade.

It was a really jolly meal. Cyril received only portion of his sardines, because Mad-dog MacTavish levied heavy toll on them. So Cyril filled up on tomatoes given him by Fish-head, who lunched sumptuously upon bread and butter, and raw onions which he ate like apples. Cyril drank his nice lemonade, but the rest of the gang, disdaining what they referred to as "Sunday School slops," washed down their repast with muddy tea, which they pronounced as delicious.

The meal over, it was resolved unanimously not to go trapping that afternoon, but to laze around the tent. Fishhead had made the discovery that the waterhole was teeming with fresh-water yabbies, so, armed with a length of string and a piece of bacon supplied by Cyril without his knowledge, he prepared to fish for them. As a preliminary he placed the billy can filled with water on the fire. Yabby angling was good, and as Fish-head landed them he tossed them into the boiling billy. When he had secured sufficient and had cooked them thoroughly, he shelled them and ate them like prawns. He would eat practically anything, would young Mr. Barker.

Late in the afternoon, when the six boys were sitting inside the tent discussing plans for the night and the morrow, their attention was called to the behaviour of the double-bar finch in the bird trap outside. This trap, and that containing the redhead, or fire-tailed finch, had been left on top of an old stump. The redhead was quiet, but the double-bar was chirping loudly. Silence fell on the six boys, and as they listened to the little finch in the trap they heard the chirping of others.

"Don't make a row, boys," whispered Spider Webb. "I think there's a mob of double-bars not far away. Keep still and I'll take a gander around."

Crawling from the tent on his hands and knees, he peered in the direction from where the chirping had come. For a moment he saw and heard nothing more, but then his eye caught some movement in a bush about a hundred yards away. Then he saw a bird drop from the bush into the grass. Undoubtedly it was a double-bar. He waited until he saw a few other birds join the first one on the ground and then crawled back into the tent and told the rest of the gang.

"What we have to do is to sneak that trap off the stump without disturbing the double-bars and shove it near one of the bushes away from the tent. They won't come nearer here, you can bet on that. Next we will circle around and drive them towards the trap—you know, the same old routine," said Spider. The others nodded. With the exception of Cyril, they were all experienced bird trappers.

"You blokes stay here and I'll see what I can do," Spider continued. "I'll get the double-bar trap and cart it up past the tent in the opposite direction. I'll find a good spot for it and then I'll come back. Okay?" Again the gang nodded silently. They knew they could trust Spider to do the job efficiently and well.

Spider crawled out of the tent again, and across to the stump. Reaching up, he secured the trap and then crawled with it into the scrub which was only a few yards away. Once there, he stood up and made his way silently through the bushes until he reached a lone shrub about 200 yards past the tent. Here he set the trap and returned by the same route to the scrub opposite the tent. Before going any further, he had a quick look towards the spot where he had seen the flock of of double-bars. He could see some of them hopping around on the ground and could hear their chirping. He stole quietly hack into the tent, picking up the redhead trap from the stump as he did so. He intended to leave this in the care of Cyril.

"Now, gang," he said, "we've got to drive the flock past this tent and up to near the trap. The caller will do the rest. I guess two of us will be enough, eh?"

"Yep," said Fish-head. "You've done a good job, Spider, and have earned a break. Whizzer and me will now take over. The rest of you lay low and don't make a row. Come on, Whizzer."

The two boys passed silently from the tent and into the scrub beyond. They dived deeper into the bush and began a wide circle to get behind the double-bars. This proved easy enough. And when they came in sight of the flock, some of which were in the grass and some in the bushes, they commenced to walk slowly towards them. The little birds, seeing them approach, immediately became alarmed and took to the bushes. And as the two boys advanced cautiously, so did the finches retreat, hopping and flitting from bush to bush towards the tent. Soon they were near the tent, then past it, flitting in the right direction. Fish-head and Whizzer could not pick out individual birds or guess at the number in the flock, but they were not concerned with that. The hunt was going well.

The four boys in the tent remained in deathly silence as the flock passed not more than a dozen feet in front of them. Breathlessly they watched the birds go by.

Suddenly Cyril gave a short gasp and grabbed Maddog MacTavish's arm.

"Did you see that bird?" he exclaimed.

"Keep quiet, you noisy coot, or you'll scare them!" hissed Mad-dog.

"Yes, but that bird isn't a double-bar finch. It's a—why, it's a canary!" cried Cyril, unable to contain himself.

"A what? A canary?" snorted Mad-dog. "Oh, don't be a fool. You're seeing things. And, for the love of Mike, keep your voice down, will you?"

"I tell you I saw a canary. It's gone by now, but it was right in the middle of the finches," said Cyril. In his excitement he jumped to his feet, but was roughly pulled back to earth by the others in the tent.

"You didn't see any canaries, you dashed goat," said Spider. "You want to get your eyes tested. That lemonade you had for lunch has gone to your head."

"I did, I tell you," cried Cyril passionately. "Don't you think I know a canary when I see one? Don't we breed them at home? I did see a canary!"

"You'll see stars if I punch you in the eye," warned Spider Webb. "Now, pipe down. Say, there goes Fishhead and Whizzer. Everything under control, Fishhead?" he said in a loud whisper. Fish-head nodded, but did not speak, and presently he and Whizzer had passed out of sight.

When he deemed it safe to move, Spider Webb signalled to the others and they all left the tent, Cyril with them. He did not like bird trapping, but he was determined to catch another glimpse of that canary, if possible. Walking in Indian file, the four lads crossed into the scrub and made their way cautiously towards the spot where the trap had been set. They had gone only a few yards when they came up to Fish-head and Whizzer who were crouched down behind a bush, from behind which they could keep the trap under observation.

Now six boys were down behind the bush, eagerly awaiting developments. The trap was on the ground a short distance away, and the double-bar caller was chirping away inside. Other chirps could be heard in the bushes ahead, and Fish-head informed the gang in a whisper that it was only a matter of time before the flock investigated the trap, attracted there by the caller. Then things would occur.

"This goat Cyril reckons he saw a canary among the double-bars as they flew past the tent," Mad-dog confided to Fish-head in an undertone. "Did you see anything that looked like a canary?"

"A canary? Oh, don't be daft! What the heck would a canary be doing in a flock of double-bar finches?" chuckled Fish-head.

"Well, I saw one," said Cyril sulkily.

"Never noticed it myself. Saw a few white cockatoos and half a dozen emus, but not a canary," said Fishhead, who was something of a humorist.

Cyril saw that it was a waste of time arguing with that gang of unbelievers, so, wisely, he held his peace.

"Hey, there they go!" hissed Spider Webb.

Several finches had dropped to the ground from the bushes and were hopping around near the trap. This contrivance had four hinged doors, each held back by a twig. Should a bird hop down on to the twig to reach the seed thoughtfully scattered on the floor underneath, the twig would fall under its weight and the bird would be held prisoner. None of the finches seemed disposed to hop on top of the trap. They gathered around it and communed for a second or two with their imprisoned colleague, but nothing else.

"Hey, what was that?" was the sudden exclamation of Whizzer Perrett. "What was that bird that jumped out of the bushes? Look, to the right of the trap. Looks like a sparrow!"

"It is undoubtedly a canary," said Cyril quietly. "Or perhaps I am mistaken and it is an emu, or a white cockatoo."

"By the holy, pink-toed tiger snake, it is a canary!" exclaimed Whizzer Perrett. "Well, stone the blinking nanny goats! What the heck is a canary doing there?"

"Never mind what it is doing there. Keep your big mouths shut and see if it goes into the trap," admonished Fish-head.

"If we catch it, it's mine, because I own the trap," said Spider Webb loudly.

"That's what you think, Spider," said Fish-head. "We'll toss for it."

"Oh, no, we won't," declared Spider. "It's my trap and my

caller and my bird seed. Therefore, it's my canary."

"Suppose we wait until it's trapped?" suggested Skinny O'Neill. "Now all of you shut up and watch."

What the lads were watching was, indeed, a canary, and a very dirty and dilapidated one. Boofie had been with the double-bars for several days now, and was enjoying the peaceful and mildly-adventurous life. His cage days were completely forgotten. To all intents and purposes he was a double-bar finch and a welcome member of that gentle little community. His habit of washing in dirty mudholes had not improved his appearance. He needed a good clean-up.

When the finches were in the bushes, Boofie was always the last one to leave when the flock took to the ground to feed; that was why he had lingered behind when the rest of his friends had dropped down near the trap. Boofie inspected the contrivance curiously. Vaguely it reminded him of something in his past life. The wires brought back dim memories. He associated them somehow with canary seed—something he had not eaten for a week or so. From the ground he hopped on top of the trap and peered over the edge. On the floor he saw canary seed! Eagerly he hopped on to the convenient perch. There was a loud bang, and next moment he was on the floor, the perch still in his claws. Strange, he thought, and then forgot everything in his eagerness to eat up as much of the seed as he could. This was fine!

Back in the bushes, Fish-head was hard put to it restraining the rest of the gang from rushing madly to the trap. He told them to stay where they were, pointing out that there were still three doors unsprung, and the double-bars were still around. The sound of the closing trapdoor had startled them a little, but had not dispersed them. The canary was safely caught, and there was a chance that they could pick up a double-bar or two also.

"There *was* a canary among the finches," said Cyril. "I knew

I was not mistaken. I am not the fool you boys think I am."
Nobody answered him.

Boofie, having finished all the seed in the compartment, decided
to rejoin his friends, the double-bars. In another compartment
he noticed one of the finches, and chirped to it an invitation to
come along with him. The finch chirped back, but did nothing.
It couldn't. Neither could Boofie, a fact he soon discovered.

And when he realised that once again he was confined by
wires, he put on an act that quite outdid any he had ever staged
in the cage at the Westwood home. He had hardly enough space
in which to turn round, and he lost his head completely, dashing
himself against the wires, getting his wings tangled in corners,
hanging upside down from the trap roof and generally giving way
to panic. It did him no good, but it did a service to the flock of
double-bars. These birds, alarmed by the commotion in the trap,
took to the bushes and vanished into the thick scrub.

"It's not much use trying to round them up again this arvo,"
commented Fish-head "Let's collect the trap and have a dekko
at this canary."

He led the excited rush of boys towards the trap. Spider Webb
beat him to it and, holding it aloft, examined the prisoner. The
rest of the gang crowded around him.

"H'm, not much of a catch," commented Mad-dog MacTavish.
"That thing wouldn't win a prize in a show."

"Let me see it," said Cyril, peering closely at Boofie. "Plain
yellow, with a black patch on the back of the head and a touch
of buff on a wing. It's a Border Fancy, and a very ordinary one."

"Not quite up to the standard of yours, eh, Butch?" grinned
Whizzer Perrett.

"Well, all of our birds are show exhibits," replied Cyril. "Our
Border Fancies, Yorkshires and Norwiches are all pure, and . . . "

"Some other time," interrupted Fish-head impatiently. "I say,

Whizzer, I wonder if this joker is the same that we hunted around the School of Arts last week? Looks a bit like it."

"I guess not," said Whizzer. "If that thing got out of the hall it will be dead by now. The cats will have chewed it up."

"Sure. Okay, boys, let's get back to the tent. Tomorrow we might be able to round up that flock of doublebars again. Or we might try for some redheads."

"I know a whacko place for redheads," said Skinny O'Neill.

"You know a whacko place for nothing," interrupted Fish-head coldly. "You and your bush stuffed tight with birds. Shut up."

"Don't you mugs start that argument again," said Spider Webb. "Come back to the tent."

Triumphantly he led the way, the trap with Boofie in it held out in front of him like a torch. At the tent, the trap was replaced on the stump with the redhead trap on top of it, and the gang set about preparing its evening banquet. This time Cyril's ample stock of provisions was drawn upon. Bacon and eggs were fried with onions and tomatoes, tins of preserved fruit were opened and bottles of cordials dispensed.

CHAPTER NINE

Ghostly Goings On!

BOOFIE settled down peacefully in the trap. He had spent all his previous life in prison and was used to restricted quarters, although this cage was the smallest he had even been in. He felt like a drink of water, and this was provided by Cyril Gorton, who thoughtfully placed some in the lid of a tin and put it in a spare compartment of the trap, giving both Boofie and the doublebar access to it by removing the wire pins in between. He also did a like service for the redhead in the second trap and gave all three birds some more seed.

It was getting near sundown when all the gang congregated in the tent for a yarn, leaving the traps outside on the stump. They were discussing the events of the day and quarrelling over the ultimate ownership of the canary, when there was a commotion in the traps. As the boys watched, they saw the two finches fluttering madly in their respective compartments. Boofie was hopping around in his cell, but did not appear to be in the same state of agitation.

"What the heck is up with them?" asked Spider Webb. "They're gone mad all of a sudden. I'd better go and bring them inside the tent."

He was on the point of carrying out his design, when a loud but very musical bird call rang out. This made the finches redouble their panicky flutterings. Suddenly there came a rush of wings, and out of the top of a stringybark darted a large, handsome silver-grey bird with a black cap and throat and a cruelly hooked beak. It dived straight at the traps and, landing on the tree stump, thrust its beak in between the wires. The terror-stricken little double-bar and redhead united their shrill voices with the excited chirpings of the canary, as the big bird, hopping on top of the trap, tore at the wires with its cruel bill.

"Butcher bird!" yelled Spider Webb, dashing from the tent. "Get away, you brute! Leave those birds alone, dash you!"

The butcher bird heard him and made to escape, but its claws were tangled in the wire of the top trap-that containing Boofie and the double-bar, and as it went to fly away it upset the trap, which fell to the ground on the opposite side of the stump. With a loud and defiant squawk, the marauder fled into the treetops, while Spider Webb shouted abuse and insults at it. Then, as the rest of the gang crowded from the tent, he walked around the stump and picked up the fallen trap.

And when he did pick it up he began to use rather deplorable language. The double-bar was inside, dead. Of Boofie there was no sign. The wires that had been torn aside by the talons of the butcher bird provided a clue to what had happened. The canary had made good its escape through the gaping hole, and heaven alone knew where it was now.

There were loud lamentations about it. Instead of three birds, the trappers now possessed only one—the redhead.

"I wonder if that useless butcher bird got the canary?" pondered Whizzer. "It could have. We didn't see all that happened."

"No, I think the canary got out through the hole in the wire when the cage was knocked over. That is what probably killed the double-bar, unless the butcher bird got in a crack with its beak," said Fish-head.

"Butcher birds," said Cyril with the air of a lecturer, "are notorious for the way in which they raid cages and pull the heads and legs from birds as they flutter against the wires. We would have found the canary's body if that had happened. Doubtless it has escaped, and is now safely at large in the bush."

Boofie was at large in the bush, all right, but whether he was safe was a debatable question. When the trap had hit the ground he had found himself half out of the hole in the wire. Wriggling through, he had flittered into the scrub without being seen, and was now perched fearfully on a twig in the heart of a thick acacia bush, wishing that his old friends, the double-bar flock, were near. But they were miles away in the bush, preparing to go to roost. After a while the philosophical Boofie gave himself a sketchy preening and went to roost himself—on the same acacia twig. Almost as philosophically, the Black Star Gang, in the tent, settled down again for a yarn. It was useless crying over spilled milk, or escaped birds, as Skinny O'Neill remarked wisely.

"It is just as well we lost that canary," remarked Spider Webb. "First of all, it would only have started a brawl among us about who was going to own the thing, and, anyway, they are too much of of a nuisance to keep. They are always getting sick and have to be looked after and put to bed at night like dashed babies."

"That is not strictly accurate," said Cyril. "Certainly they take a great deal of care, especially when they are breeding, but a single bird in a cage needs only proper food and clean water daily.

"Really, it is a most fascinating hobby," he went on with enthusiasm, disregarding the amused looks on the faces of the other boys as they gave him an indulgent hearing. "I love to watch them bustling around, making their nests, then waiting anxiously for the eggs to be laid and the youngsters hatched. Then there is another most anxious period—ensuring that the parent birds feed the nestlings regularly and properly. They do not always do so, you know."

"Ah, that's where Cirry takes over," grinned Mad-dog. "I'd give a couple of quid to see Cirry with a mouthful of chewed-up grass hopping about on the perches feeding the young 'uns."

"Haw, haw, haw!" laughed Fish-head raucously. "Sweet, pretty joey! Scratch cocky's comb with a crowbar!"

"One does not feed the young on grass," said Cyril patiently. "One supplies the birds with the yolks of hard-boiled eggs, and the parents feed the young with this. If they don't, then we feed them, using the egg somewhat like cream, and giving it to them, using an eye-dropper or a small syringe. It is indeed a worrying time. We do not always succeed in rearing them, you know."

"And how long does this business take?" demanded Mad-dog. "Seems to me Spider was right when he said they're a darned nuisance."

"No, it is most fascinating," said Cyril. "After the hen lays the eggs, it takes ten or eleven days for them to hatch and then about three weeks before the young are fully feathered and ready to leave the nest. Give them plenty of right food and they are no trouble at all."

"Well, it's too much trouble for the likes of me," said Spider.

"Anyway, be that as it may, and apart from anything else," said Fish-head, upon whom the canary lecture was beginning to pall, "as leader of this expedition, it is up to me to make arrangements for tonight. I propose that each one of us goes on guard duty for one hour right through until two o'clock in the morning, in case some of the smart guys from the town have found out where we are and want to get up to some funny business. It is now six o'clock and it won't be dark until nearly seven. We won't need a sentry until eight o'clock at the earliest. I'll do the first hour, Whizzer the second, then Mad-dog, Skinny and Spider. That will take us up to 1 a.m. I'll go on again then for the last hour. We'll leave Cyril off duty as he has done enough around the camp today. You jokers agree to all this?"

Except for Cyril, the rest of the gang intimated their acceptance of the arrangements. Cyril stated that he would be proud to share in the protection of the camp and would deem it a great favour if he were permitted to do sentry duty for the last hour, from 1 a.m. to 2 a.m. It would be great fun.

"Good for you, Butch," commended Fish-head. "Then that's settled. Now. It is just as well to go armed in case we get any visitors. I've got my airgun, so I'm set. The rest of you birds had better get yourselves a thick waddy from the bush. While you are on sentry duty you have my airgun."

"What will we use for bullets?" Spider Webb wanted to know.

"I've got a tin of airgun shot, but a charge of spud is as good as anything, and it can hurt all right," replied Fish-head. "All you jokers know how to load up with spud, don't you?"

Cyril didn't, so Fish-head showed him how to extract the dart chamber from the barrel and plunge the end of it into a potato. When the dart chamber was replaced in the gun, half an inch of "spud" was ready to be discharged at an enemy. Except for Fish-head, the rest of the gang then scattered into the bush, presently to return armed with thick sticks.

Punctually at eight o'clock by Cyril's watch—none of the others possessed a timekeeper—Fish-head, his rifle at the slope, left the tent and began to march up and down outside, like, as Mad-dog MacTavish remarked, a cockatoo on stilts. The rest of the mob sat in the tent and played cards, Cyril looking on.

Fish-head had been on guard for perhaps ten minutes, when he poked his head into the tent and stated that the fire was getting low. More wood was needed. He was told promptly to go and get it himself. He refused. There was, he said, no provision in military regulations about sentries knocking off guard duty and getting firewood. It would, he said, be lovely, if the Grenadier Guards or the other blokes on duty outside Buckingham Palace had to leave off keeping an eye out for the Queen's enemies to rush around London searching for hunks of dashed wood. The guard would be shot at dawn and his body chucked into the River Thames.

"And if some of you lazy coots don't go and gather up some wood and keep that dashed fire going." he wound up darkly, "some of you will collect a charge of spud from my gun and be chucked into that dirty waterhole over there, in which waterhole I have got some yabby lines set. Get me?"

The Black Star Gang intimated, in offensive voices, that they understood him, and then resumed their cardplaying.

"So it's gonna be mutiny, is it?" growled Fish-head. "All right, you jokers, you asked for it. Cop this!" Saying which, he levelled his gun at Spider Webb, who promptly ducked.

"Oh, no, don't shoot, Benjamin," pleaded Cyril. "I'll get the wood."

"You stay where you are, Butch," said Fish-head, training his gun on Mad-dog MacTavish. "You've done enough around here. It's time these others did a bit. Get going, Mad-dog."

"Oh, for the love of Mike, Fish-head." said Skinny O'Neill irritably, "get lost. You give me the ginger willies. Go and play soldiers and leave us alone. Do you think you're the king pin ..." He broke off with an agonised yelp as a charge of potato caught him on the bare leg. "Hey, Fish-head, you dopy-looking thing, that hurt!"

"It was meant to hurt," snorted Fish-head, whipping the dart chamber from the gun barrel and plunging the end into a piece of potato he had. "The rest of you beauts will cop the same unless you obey orders. Get a move on."

"I'll see you dead and buried before I'll get any dashed wood," howled Skinny O'Neill, feverishly massaging his wounded leg. "For two pins I'd crack you one, you murdering devil."

"Not while I'm able to use this gun, you won't," retorted Fish-head, covering the recalcitrant Skinny with the weapon.

"I'll get the wood," said Cyril hurriedly. "I'll go." And before anyone could stop him—not that any move was made to do so—he was out of the tent and hurrying into the dark bush.

"You jokers make me sick the way you impose on that kid," said Fish-head.

"Look who's talking," scoffed Mad-dog. "You're the worst

of the lot. Anyway, he's not a kid. He's older than me. I'm only eleven and he must be thirteen if he's a minute."

"Almost a grandfather. Well, cut it out and give him a break," grunted Fish-head, as he shouldered his trusty gun and resumed his sentry beat.

Cyril rather enjoyed the novelty of being in the bush in the dark, with the cheery glow of the campfire to guide him back. He gave himself a thrill by imagining that the gloomy bush was peopled with demons and ghosts. A bush, rustling in the slight breeze, made him catch his breath with terror so, hastily grabbing a few sticks, he hurried back towards the tent. In sight of the glowing fire and the picture of Fish-head marching up and down, his courage returned to him and he smiled to himself as a plan entered his head. He would make a noise to see if Benjamin were really on the alert. Benjamin was, as Cyril found out.

"Woo, woo, woo!" he called in a voice he fondly imagined was that of an owl.

"Who goes there?" roared Fish-head, pointing his gun at the darkness.

"Woo, woo, wool" chortled Cyril, giving an encore.

"Bang!" went the airgun, and Cyril yelped like a stricken bull-pup as the charge of potato got him fairly on the lobe of the left ear. Dropping his bundle of sticks, he hopped up and down like a wounded frog, his left hand clasped to his stinging ear. And the howls he uttered were quite astonishing.

"Who goes there?" bellowed Fish-head again, as he reloaded the airgun with practised precision. "Come on, show your ugly mug before you stop another slug."

"Don't shoot!" came an anguished cry from the bushes. "It's me, Cyril Gorton. You nearly shot my eye out."

"Serves you right for acting the goat," said Fish-head, unsympathetically. "Now cut out the funny business and bring that wood back to the fire. The thing's nearly out."

Poor Cyril, his ear stinging like anything, gathered up the sticks and brought them to the fire. He stacked them in a neat heap and then placed a few on the blaze.

"I'm surprised at you, dinkum I am," said Fish-head sternly. "You might have lost your eyesight, acting the fool and making noises like that. I'm sorry I shot you in the eye, but a sentry must always be on the alert and do his duty."

"You hit me on the ear, not the eye, and it hurts very much," replied Cyril, tears in his eyes.

"In the ear?" snorted the sentry. "Gosh, that's a mile off your eye. I'm ashamed of you, telling me foul lies like that, Cirry."

Disdaining to answer these shafts of satire, Cyril returned to the bush and presently came back with more wood. He made three other trips before he finally retired to the tent. He refused to speak a word to Fish-head. He was not pleased with him. As for Fish-head, he couldn't care less what Cyril thought about him.

Not long after this occurrence, Fish-head handed his gun and potato over to Whiner Perrett, and joined the gang in the tent. Whizzer in turn, at 10 p.m., handed over to Mad-dog MacTavish. And it was during Maddog's watch that an incident took place.

Young Mr. MacTavish was marching up and down in approved fashion when, chancing to glance across the clearing beyond the tent, he noticed a slight movement. He came to a halt and watched it. Soon the object became clearer—it was a white figure and it was waving its arms about.

"That looks like a girl," Mad-dog muttered, forgetting to issue the time-honoured challenge. "This wants looking into. We don't want any chooks hanging around here."

"Who goes there?" he asked, in a voice scarcely above a whisper. There was no reaction from the ghostly figure, so Mad-dog repeated his question in a louder tone.

The figure made no verbal reply, but rattled a length of bullock chain.

"Strike!" murmured Mad-dog. "That looks like a ghost." He raised the airgun and levelled it at the figure, but could not take aim because he was trembling like an under-set jelly. Ghosts, anyway, could not be mown down with potato fired from an airgun. And, after all, it might really be a girl.

"Is t-t-that you, J-J-Josie Bub-bub-Bourke?" he stuttered.

"Wh-o-o-o-o-o!" yelled the so-called Miss Bourke, and that was more than sufficient for young Mr. MacTavish. With a howl of fright he dashed into the tent, fell over Cyril and quite inadvertently dug the airgun into Fishhead's stomach. The gang, which was still playing cards, looked at him with wild surmise.

"What the dickens is wrong with you?" howled Fishhead, massaging his stomach. "Have you gone mad all of a sudden?"

"Ghosts!" screamed Mad-dog wildly. "Dirty big ghosts with sheets all over them! Come outside and see!"

Taking their waddies for protection, the mob streamed out of the tent, and Mad-dog, with a shaking finger, indicated the mysterious white figure.

"Who are you?" shouted Fish-head. "Come over here and give us a look at you."

The ghost responded by hopping around like a monkey doing the samba, at the same time rattling the chain and uttering a weird howl. Cyril Gorton, unused to such supernatural manifestations, grizzled with fright.

"Shut up, you!" ordered Fish-head in a trembling voice as he dealt Cyril a smart slap on the side of the face. Cyril's grizzle developed into a full-throated howl.

"Let's charge it all together," suggested Skinny O'Neill, getting behind Whizzer Perrett.

"Charge it yourself," whimpered Mad-dog MacTavish. "I wish I was home."

"Come on, Black Star Gang!" bellowed Fish-head bravely as he waved his airgun around his head. He made a rush at the ghost and the rest of the gang, keeping tight hands on their waddies, followed like sheep. Cyril, however, rushed into the tent and shoved his head under a heap of blankets.

Howling like banshees to keep their spirits up, the gang took after the alleged ghost, which dropped its chain and rushed off into the darkness. Skinny O'Neill, the fastest runner among the hunters, was the first to catch up with it, and he stuck his waddy between its legs, tripping it and bringing it crashing to earth. As it fell, he brought his waddy down on its head with a sickening thud. The ghost howled like mad. The rest of the brave warriors, especially Fish-head Barker, began to hit and kick the unfortunate phantom until it looked as if it might be deprived of its life. It was Spider Webb who solved the mystery by ripping off the sheet in which the howling figure was entangled. It was his brother Herbie, a young gentleman two years older.

"Ho, so it's you, Cocky Webb, is it?" roared Fishhead. "What's the strength of this funny business?"

Herbie Webb, alias Cocky, who was black and blue from the bashing he had received, was in no mood for arguments or explanations. He hauled himself to his feet, the tears streaming down his face, and he proceeded to say a lot to Fish-head—all uncomplimentary. He then addressed the rest of the gang in similar terms. The gist of his remarks was that they were a pack of murderous hooligans, they had nearly killed him, he'd tell the police, his father, Fish-head's father, and, if necessary, send a petition to the Queen. He broke off his tirade to howl.

"Clear out before you cop some more," ordered Fishhead. "You got what you deserved, coming here and trying to frighten us by acting as a ghost. Now shoot through or I'll bash you up again."

"There's more days than one, Fish-head!" howled Cocky. "Just you wait, the lot of you. As for you, Spider, you wait till I get home and tell the old man on you. You'll cop it."

"On your way, Cocky," directed Fish-head. "And if you make

trouble at home for Spider, the Black Star Gang will fix you for good. Now don't you forget that."

Cocky Webb again expressed his opinion of the Black Star Gang, repeating all he had said previously, and adding a few more ill-chosen epithets. The gang heard him out without much comment.

"Oh, Cocky, just before you go. Here's a little token of our love," said Fish-head, diving his hand into his pocket and producing a crude black star. "Our visiting card."

Cocky took one look at the card and one look at Fish-head. He opened his mouth to say something, thought better of it, and then limped away howling into the night.

Back to the tent went the valorous gang to celebrate its victory. Five of them, armed with nothing better than sticks and an airgun, had successfully vanquished one lone, unarmed boy swathed in a sheet. It was a heartening thought. Victoria Crosses had been awarded for less! The celebration took the form of a comprehensive raid upon what was left of Cyril's provisions. Everything except a special tin of preserved peaches which Cyril had hidden under his bed, was turned into a feast, and to this the gang gave its undivided attention. It was considered unnecessary to mount guard any more.

The feast was at its height when, from out of the night, there came a plaintive voice calling for its "dear little Cyril."

"Now, what?" spluttered Fish-head, his mouth stuffed with raw onion.

"That is mother. I wonder what she wants?" exclaimed Cyril. "Here I am, mother, dear," he added, raising his voice. He ran out of the tent, the gang following at a slower pace. Sure enough, there was Mrs. Gorton, accompanied by the wounded Herbie Webb and another person whom the gang identified as Froggie Fitzpatrick. (He had been given the Christian name of Bernard.)

"What's crawling on you, missus?" demanded Fishhead of Mrs. Gorton. "And what are these other mugs doing here? I thought I told you to go home, Cocky?"

"Shut your face, Fish-head," replied Cocky Webb. "You're in for it, and no error."

"Cyril, I want you to come home with me at once," moaned Mrs. Gorton, coldly ignoring the polite Fishhead.

"But what is the trouble, mother?" asked Cyril. "You said I could stay out all night camping with my friends."

"Yes, I did, my dear little lad, but now I want you to come home with your lonely old mother," she replied, and Cyril's top lip dropped like a motherless foal's.

"I won't come home, so there!" he exclaimed, stamping his foot.

"That's the stuff to give the troops!" said that outlaw Fish-head approvingly. "These other birds can whizz off, though. Clear out, Froggie and Cocky, and take the old chook with you."

"The larrikins are just as bad as you said they were, Bernard," said Mrs. Gorton to Froggie. "I could not credit you when you described them to me. Now I have had personal proof and I shall inform the police when I return home."

"Inform the police about what, missus?" asked Fishhead. "I don't get the strength of all this."

"It's nothing to what you will get, Fish-head," said Froggie Fitzpatrick darkly. "You've all got a lot coming to you."

"I shall explain," said Mrs. Gorton. "I had been worried about Cyril being out all night. I decided to look for him and bring him home. I met Bernard in the street and he said he would accompany me and help me find this camp. Then we heard Herbert Webb, and after what he told us of the sheer hooliganism displayed towards him earlier, we all hastened here. Herbert is badly injured, yet the brave lad volunteered to show us where the camp was. Otherwise we might have had to search for it for hours. What a brave little man he is!"

"Brave little man, me number ten foot!" grunted Whizzer Perrett.

"Just you wait till we get you alone, Cocky," said Fish-head glaring balefully at young Webb. "You'll wish you had never been born."

"Cyril," said Mrs. Gorton, ignoring this by-play, "pick up your property and let us return home. Come on now, hurry, it is very, very late."

"I hate to defy you, mother," said Cyril quietly, "but I am not going. You promised me that I could remain with my friends all night and I am going to. I never get much fun."

"Your friends?" screamed Mrs. Gorton, "Don't dare to call these hoodlums and larrikins and hooligans your friends! They should all be in prison. And if you defy me again I shall chastise you."

"I'll get him!" shouted Cocky Webb, who was tired of all the talking and wanted to go home and anoint his wounds. Froggie Fitzpatrick, however, was before him. He made a rush at Cyril, but Mad-dog MacTavish put out his foot in the darkness, and Froggie nose-dived into the waterhole, the existence of which had been completely forgotten in the excitement.

"Hey, stiffen the crows! I've got lines set in there, and you're disturbing my yabbies!" howled Fish-head Barker, dancing around the waterhole in rage.

Mrs. Gordon moaned, Fish-head bellowed, Cyril whimpered, and Mad-dog laughed like an insane kookaburra. Froggie hauled himself from the hole, spat out a mouthful of muddy water and, turning to Mrs. Gorton, remarked with unnecessary impoliteness: "You and your silly son can go and fry your faces. Come, on, Cocky, let's get out of this madhouse."

Accompanied by Cocky Webb, Froggie rushed dripping into the darkness. Slowly and sadly Cyril gathered up his belongings under the silent scrutiny of the Black Star Gang, loaded up his billy cart, took a sad farewell of his dear little playmates and departed in tears.

CHAPTER TEN

Bush Adventure

BOOFIE spent an uneventful night roosting in a dense thicket of prickly bushes covered with blackberry vines. This thicket was the favourite haunt of a family of fairy wrens—dainty little birds with long, jaunty tails who never ventured far from the dense undergrowth in which they felt safe to build their nests, to lay their eggs and to rear their young ones.

The first streaks of dawn in the eastern sky awakened all the bush birds, Boofie among them, and though the wrens—Bluecap and his family of five—immediately commenced searching for their breakfasts of insects, Boofie did nothing. He felt lost without the company of the double-bar flock, upon which he had come to depend a great deal. The finches knew where to find seeds and Boofie had profited by their knowledge. The blue wrens had nothing to do with him and, in any case, their type of meal would make no appeal to the canary. Boofie could not eat insects.

For want of something to do, Boofie, as the first glorious rays of the sun were converting into diamonds the dewdrops that still lingered on the leaves and grass, performed his toilet. It rarely varied.

Standing on the twig on his left leg, he wound his right leg round under his right wing and scratched the right side of his head with his right claws; then he stood on his left leg and did precisely the same with his left claws. Next, he explored the feathers on his right side with his beak and then the left side; then his chest and belly feathers. For a second or two after that he stood on one leg and yawned a few times. Then, with his right leg he stretched out his right wing to its full length, nearly falling over as he did so, immediately performing a similar manoeuvre with his left leg and wing. Having chirped a few times, he lifted his right wing and peered under it, gave it a few pecks and did the same with his left wing; after nearly twisting his head off to get at his tail, he gave that up, ran a few wing feathers through his bill, fluffed out all his plumage, and stood on one leg, the other disappearing into his belly feathers. A few lazy chirps, and then he settled down.

Around him, the whole bush was busy. Life for the wild creatures was one perpetual hunt for food, and though Boofie had been free for a week or more and, during his association with the double-bar finches, had managed to keep himself alive by his own efforts, he was far from being independent. Every time he awakened each morning he expected to find a tin of seed handy.

For Boofie, though he was one of Nature's creations— for only Nature had the secret of creating life—he was the product, the development, of Man. So were his ancestors for hundreds of years. Boofie, like all domesticated canaries, was a descendant of certain small green and brown finches native to the Canary Islands of the Atlantic Ocean, Madeira and the Azores. Wandering European sailors away back in the 16th century were attracted by the gay songs of the little canary finches and took them back to Italy, to Spain and to England in large numbers. Then, over the long years, Man with his patience and his skill, using artificial selection for breeding purposes, developed so many varieties and colours, that it seemed incredible of belief that they could have originated from the little green finches of the Atlantic islands. But it was so. And Man took them to every part of the world—to the mansions of the mighty, to the miserable hovels of the poor.

Man's experiments had made yellow the predominant colour of their domesticated pets, but he went further, and produced white birds, grey and white ones, even blue ones—and he even retained the original green. Man, too, had learned a trick of colour.

By feeding his canaries with a certain sweet red pepper which came from Spain, he caused yellow birds to turn deep orange and buff ones to become peach. This he did while the birds were moulting. They ate this colour-food and when the new feathers appeared they were of this new shade. But Nature here rebelled and insisted on her rights; for in this colour-feeding Man did not triumph—and has not yet. If he failed to keep up the colour-feeding, when the canaries again moulted, their coats reverted to the original yellow and buff.

Not content with keeping his canaries the one size, Man produced larger ones and smaller ones. He produced speckled or lizard-coloured birds with gold caps; and he produced some with feathered crests and others with humps on their backs.

And because these modern canaries—these descendants, over 400 years, of wild finches, had been so changed and altered and experimented with, they were quite unable and unfitted to battle for themselves in the open and free world. They were the product of Man, and dependent upon him for their existence. If it were cruel and unnatural to keep wild birds in cages, it were cruel and unnatural *not* to keep domesticated canaries in captivity. For, in creating his pets and usurping the functions of Nature, Man had made himself responsible to Nature for the life she had bestowed upon his creations.

Boofie's hunger increased to such an extent that he had to do something about it. Apparently nobody was going to bring him a tin of seed, a dish of water or a thistle, so he had to find his own food or go without.

Leaving the blackberry thicket. He flitted through the bushes and presently arrived at a patch of scrub where he had once congregated with the double-bars. Those birds were nowhere in sight. They had retired to distant parts.

Boofie flew from an acacia bush into the grass and made a light meal from seeding plants. The tuffed grass was thick hereabouts, and hard going for a canary unused to such conditions.

He was hopping around the base of a big tuft when he came beak to beak with a neat-looking little grey bird as big as himself. It pulled up in some surprise on seeing the canary. It was a pipit or ground lark, and it had a mate on a nest nearby—a deep, cup-shaped structure in a hollow near a grass tuft. The pipit had been out in the open country since dawn and was now returning home to see how its domestic affairs were progressing. Like all his kin. He did not do much flying, although he could, and did, soar to great heights when he felt in the mood. He preferred to run over the short grass of a paddock looking for insects, moving in short rushes-a few yards' trot, a pause and a swing of the body, and then another short run. He had flown to the edge of this thick grass and then had dropped to earth to continue his journey on foot. That was more in the nature of a precaution, because he did not want his movements—or the site of his nest—to be seen by any wandering birds of prey.

Boofie did not know what to make of the lark and neither did the lark know what to make of Boofie. So for a moment or two they just eyed each other with mutual distrust before the lark, skirting the canary. Passed on and vanished into the long grass. Boofie was content to let him go. He did not linger long himself among the grasses, but presently returned to the scrub.

He was drowsing among the twigs and leaves when he heard a chorus of low, plaintive whistles and a number of small birds swept into the low bushes. They were greenish-brown with greyish vests, red beaks, brows and tails—popular birds, known among human trappers as "redheads." They saw Boofie, of course, but paid no heed to him. In them, Boofie saw dimly his old friends the double-bars, though neither species looked alike, and he was disposed to chum up with them. The redheads, however, attended strictly to their own business, which, at that moment, was merely perching among the low scrub and chirping to each other.

When, one by one, they began to drop to the ground, Boofie went with them. The redheads fossicked among the leaves and grass looking for seeds and berries and Boofie fossicked with them. They did not mind.

Aloft in the sky above, a wandering duck hawk, or little falcon, saw them with satisfaction. Duck hawk was recognised as being the strongest and boldest for his size of all the Australian hawks, faster even than his kinsmen the noble and famed peregrine falcon. High above the grasslands he observed the flock of redheads feeding, and decided to do something about it. He could have pounced upon them unawares, but that was not his style. Duck hawk did not believe in grabbing birds when they were feeding or resting on the ground like some other hawks and butcher birds did. Neither did he believe in stealing helpless nestlings like the crows, the currawongs, the kookaburras and others of similar ilk. Duck hawk gave his prey a sporting chance and captured it on the wing.

He dropped down lower with the intention of flushing the flock of redheads and grabbing one, maybe two, before they could get back to the safety of the thick scrub.

It was Boofie's very ignorance of the ways of the wild that saved him from extinction. The bush-wise finches, ever alert for enemies of all kinds, became aware of the hawk's presence and panicked. With shrill cries they dashed in all directions, some making for the trees and others rushing across the open country. Boofie, who had not the faintest idea what was going on, stayed on the ground. Had he risen the hawk no doubt would have selected him for a meal, because he was the biggest bird —and the worst flier—in the flock. But Boofie, through ignorance, did not rise, and it was a terrified little redhead who had darted away from the scrub that the hawk dived on, secured with consummate ease, and retired with it in his talons to feast on, at his leisure, in a convenient tree.

Deprived of his new friends, Boofie returned to the scrub, but did not stay there. He flitted from bush to bush and then across an open space, dropping down to a shallow waterhole to have a drink. It was more mud than water, but it was the best on offer. Then he decided to have a bath. The result was hardly attractive. It was a dirty-looking, dilapidated canary that fluttered on to the low limb of a tree to dry himself in the warm sun. It was very pleasant, too. The water may not have been the cleanest, but Boofie had enjoyed the bath. He shook himself vigorously and then commenced to give himself a really thorough preening. He needed it.

Down below on a grassy patch, a pair of magpies were busily searching for grasshoppers and other insects, overturning stones and bits of dead wood to get at the worms and crickets beneath. High in the sky above, three crows drifted lazily by, their melancholy cries of "far-ther, farther," echoing mournfully on the still morning air. They were making for the flooded areas where there was death and destruction: assured of great feasts upon the carcases of animals drowned by the mighty waters and left stranded as the floods receded.

A beautiful little bird alighted on the branch not two feet from Boofie and regarded him inquisitively. It wore an attractive coat of blue-black with a scarlet throat and waistcoat and white abdomen, and it addressed Boofie in a shrill voice: "Wit-a, wit-a, wit-a!" it remarked. Boofie did not reply. "Tang-tang-tang," said the tiny bird, changing gears. Still Boofie did not comment. This creature spoke a different language.

Brushing off the canary as being unworthy of further notice, the mistletoe-bird flew to a branch a few feet higher and there began feasting on the berries of a plant growing from the branch. The seed of that plant had been dropped on that branch years before by an ancestor of this gay little creature. It was a mistletoe—a parasite plant —and the mistletoe-birds were responsible for its spread through the bush.

This mistletoe-bird had a nest fifty feet up a tree about half a mile off. It was a beautiful creation of woven spider webs and fibre, shaped like a pear and with a slit in the side for an entrance. It was hanging from a thin twig on the tree in a place no human climber could hope to reach. There were three pure white eggs in the nest, being incubated by his sober-coloured mate. But the seeds were not for her. She had to get out and get her own meals when she felt hungry. He himself had no time—he was still looking after the first hatching. The mistletoe-bird had reared a trio of young ones and as soon as they had left the nest the mother bird had laid a second clutch of eggs. And because the first lot of triplets were too young to get their own meals, and incapable, anyway, of breaking open the hard mistletoe berries, Dad had to feed them. It was a tough job, too, because the triplets did not perch meekly in the one spot and wait for him to bring them a meal. No, they hopped and flitted around the bush, and Dad had continually to round them up to feed them.

The busy little bird, watched by the wary Boofie, seized a mistletoe berry and, after a bit of quick beak work, flew off with the seed, leaving the empty husk still hanging on the stem. Boofie looked after the departing bird and then eyed the mistletoe plant curiously. He flitted up to it and examined the hanging berries. He peeked at one, but the casing was tough and his beak made no impression on it. He tried several times, but could do no good, so had to give it up. The mistletoe-bird, of course, had his own technique. To get at the sticky mass in which the seed was buried, he simply nipped off the top of the berry, then grabbed the bottom with his beak and squeezed the seed out. Had Boofie been able to accomplish this it would not have pleased him, because he would have derived no sustenance from the thick, gummy jelly surrounding the seed. It would probably have stuck his beak together and caused him some inconvenience. That is, of course, if the seed itself had not stuck in his throat and choked him. The mistletoebirds swallowed seed and all—but they were used to it. They even fed their tiny young ones with those seeds, which were almost as big as the nestlings' own heads.

And so the day wore on. Boofie was lucky enough to find a patch of thistles down near the waterhole in which he had bathed, and though he ate a hearty meal, he did not feel really well fed. As a pet of the Westwoods, he had been used to regular meals of carefully-assorted seeds, lettuce leaves, an occasional apple core and now and then a mixture of egg and biscuit. It was a varied and balanced diet, necessary for the well-being of a canary. Since his freedom he had been getting his living as best he could and though it was keeping him alive, he was not thriving on it.

Night found him on a twig high up the same gum tree on which he had seen the mistletoe-bird. He had selected as a roosting place a bunch of thickly-leaved twigs on the end of a limb and soon after sundown his head was buried in his shoulder feathers. He did not see the rising of the full moon, nor did he heed the cries of the night birds. In his happy ignorance he knew nothing of the preying creatures of the dark hours—the owls, the nightjars, the frogmouths, the native cats, the tiger cats.

Up near the top of the tree there was a deep hole in the trunk, formed after a dead limb had fallen off years before. As the moon climbed higher, the sound of a slight scuffle might have been heard in this hollow, and presently a furred little face with a sharp nose and big, luminous eyes, protruded. The face looked out upon the bushland for a moment, then its owner emerged on to the nearby branch. And as it stood there, its long, cylindrical bushy tail hanging over the side of the branch, the animal, a glider possum, looked very beautiful indeed in its dusky black, soft, silky coat and white belly. As if to announce that the night's business was about to commence, it gave a queer gurgling hiss, developing into a cry that ran up the scale and ended in a terrific shriek. It woke Boofie, who sat for a moment peering this way and that, wondering what was going on, but after a few moments, during which the glider possum held its peace, he was reassured and replaced his head in his shoulder feathers.

Running along its branch, the possum reached a bunch of eucalyptus leaves and soon was dining off the tender young tips. Its hunger satisfied, it ran back along the branch to the trunk, down which it scampered until it reached the branch on which grew the clump of leaves housing Boofie. Here it paused for a moment, and then, turning around, galloped back up the trunk, past its home in the hollow, and paused only when it reached the last limb strong enough to bear its weight. Curling its tail around this, it dropped head downwards and began to swing to and fro like a pendulum, chattering merrily to itself as it did so. Tiring of this, it regained the limb and sat for a while studying the surrounding trees. Selecting one about fifty yards away, it suddenly launched itself from the limb, and, with its graceful body spread wide and its long tail streaming out behind, it shot downwards, aiming at the base of the other tree. Within a few yards of the bottom it suddenly volplaned upwards and, sailing in an arc, reached the trunk about six feet from the ground. Clinging to the tree with its sharp, powerful, curved claws, it gave a triumphant shriek, and then rushed up the trunk like an express train. It had, of course, been assisted in its gliding by the kite-like membranes stretched between its front and rear legs on either side of its body.

Reaching the top of the tree, the possum paused long enough to select another "landing field," and then it took off again, floating gracefully at an incline towards an ironbark over thirty feet away. It reached this and rushed up to the top, only to repeat the performance. Without pause, the little animal used quite a dozen trees in this fashion and in next to no time was more than half a mile from its home. Nature, in fashioning the glider possum or phalanger, had decreed that it live wholly in the trees, and its bodily structure had been developed with this end in view. On the ground it was very clumsy, but in the trees it was king.

The possum played around the bushland for most of the night, sometimes with friends of its own kind, and sometimes alone. It was early morning before it decided to return to its parent tree and bed down for the day. The tree was easily distinguished by the amount of tom and stripped bark lying around—the result of the phalanger's many take-offs in its gliding.

It reached the last tree to home and before launching itself had a final feed of leaves. Then, uttering its peculiar cry, it spread its body flat until it looked something like a banjo, pointed its nose at the foot of the home tree, straightened its tail, and dived. The base of the tree was perhaps 100 feet away, an easy task for the powerful little glider possum.

But it did not make it. It had hardly covered a dozen feet before a large speckled bird, with a hideous scream like the choking of an insane woman, swooped out of the tree and seized it in its talons. The terrified possum screeched to high heaven and struggled madly for its life, but it was in the clutches of a powerful owl, the biggest feathered night preyer of the Australian bush.

It was adding insult to mortal injury for the owl to take the luckless glider possum to its own home tree and use a branch thereof as a dining table, but the owl had no feelings of delicacy. It ate its meal only a few yards away from a startled canary, which, huddled in the gum leaves, had not yet recovered from the shock with which it had awakened—the shock caused by the owl's hideous screech. Boofie this time was quite aware of what going on, because he could actually see the great owl feeding off the possum. He might be an unsophisticated and domesticated canary with no knowledge of the grim law of the wild, but he had enough raw sense to know that if that owl saw him it would be his final curtain call.

But the owl did not see him. It was wholly occupied with its possum meal, and as soon as this was over it flew away on ghostly wings, and Boofie saw it no more.

CHAPTER ELEVEN

Boofie Goes Home

SINGING softly to herself as she performed the daily task she loved, Mrs. Gorton was attending to the needs of her canary family. On the wall of the back of the house. Which was roofed over but unenclosed, hung a row of cages from which issued a chorus of almost deafening song. It was towards the end of the breeding season, and she had quite a number of unflighted, or young birds, on hand. These, in due course, would be sold to approved customers.

Mrs. Gorton loved every one of her canaries, and each year she was reluctant to allow any to go out of her hands. In no circumstances would she sell a bird to a person about whose gentleness she had the slightest doubt. Unless a customer could prove to her, beyond all reasonable suspicion, that the canary would have a first-class home and be treated better than one of the family. No sale took place, and in no circumstances, either, would she sell a bird to a strange boy, even though his references were outstanding. If she could not sell a bird to a proven friend or to a person guaranteed by a proven friend, then she would not sell at all. As for selling to pet-shop dealers, the mere thought made her feel sick and faint.

At the moment she had only two pairs of birds breeding and each nest contained three well-grown fledglings. One pair were Yorkshires. Big, noble, colour-fed orange birds. And the others were Border Fancies. Smaller but more sprightly. And as she moved from cage to cage, she made little chirping noises and the bright-eyed songsters chirped back at her. They all knew her as friend and provider, and she had pet names for each of them.

"Now, then, Terry, I hope you are doing your motherly duty and feeding your youngsters correctly," she said to a tubby little yellow and buff hen that was eating mightily from a dish of hard-boiled egg-yolk. "You take that to the nest and don't eat it all yourself, you greedy little thing! See that she does, Beaky." This last remark was addressed to the cock bird, a handsome pure yellow chap, whose top beak was shorter than the bottom. This had occurred when, as a hungry youngster, he had tumbled from the nest. He would never win a prize in a show because of this deformity, but he was a first-class songster and an outstanding parent. Mrs. Gorton had had him for three years and would never part with him.

From Terry and Beaky she passed on to greet "Whitey" and "Hattie." Whitey, as his name indicated, was a white Border Fancy with a dash of buff on one wing. Hatty was yellow, with a black "hat" on her head. They were busily feeding their triplets, now out of the nest. The triplets were a variegated trio—one pure white, known to Mrs. Gorton as "Snowball," one buff with a white waistcoat, nicknamed "Sparrow," and a plain yellow chap whom she called "Pinhead" because, when he was hatched he had a long, thin neck.

The third cage contained a Yorkshire in solitary state, a magnificent orange-coloured bird with a black head. This was "The Baron," her champion colour-fed show bird. Alongside him was a large cage containing ten unnamed youngsters, all hatched that season and now able to look after themselves. They would be sold to those approved clients who could prove that they were a mixture of angel, paragon and perfection.

Having seen to the wants of the birds, Mrs. Gorton entered the house and proceeded to Cyril's room. It was still early in the morning, the sun having risen only half an hour before, but it was time Cyril bestirred himself. School had not yet reopened owing to the floods, but there were chores to be done around the home.

Having awakened the lad and instructed him to have his bath, get dressed and come to breakfast, Mrs. Gorton proceeded to prepare that meal. And as she did so she pondered over Cyril. This was not unusual, because Cyril was rarely out of her thoughts, but recently she had had cause to be perturbed.

Mrs. Gorton was not very pleased with Cyril. She still had very unpleasant memories of that night in the bush, now over a week ago, when, surrounded and egged on by his hooligan friends, he had been rude to her. That hurt very much; but there was a bright side. Cyril was no longer a member of the Black Star Gang. He had given his promise that he would drop that crowd, and she knew he would keep that promise.

When mother and son sat down to breakfast ten minutes later, Mrs. Gorton did not mention the subject. She chatted with Cyril about ordinary events, discussed the latest flood news and voiced her anxiety about the welfare of a certain canary fledgling, the daughter of Terry and Beaky, which did not seem to be progressing.

"That Terry is such a foolish little bird," Mrs. Gorton sighed. "She thinks more of eating herself than feeding the young ones. And the way she wastes seed! She thinks that the nicest seeds are at the bottom of the tin, so she thrusts her little beak right down, flicks it about and seed flies in all directions. She wastes a great deal more than she eats. Only for dear Beaky, I'm sure all the young ones would starve. He is continually at work. Poor boy, how tired he must be at the end of each day."

"Yes, mother," replied Cyril dutifully. He loved all the canaries, but did not possess the slavish devotion to them that his mother did. "It seems a harsh thing to say, but I think Terry is insane. Have you ever seen her clawing her way up and down the wire front of her cage and hanging head downwards to eat the thistles pushed into it?"

"I certainly have, and it is not correct conduct for the mother of three children!" said Mrs. Gorton severely.

"Certainly not!" said Cyril, smiling to himself.

"After breakfast," his mother went on, "I'd like you to fix the hose to the tap for me. I must water the back garden. How dry things are! One would not think that we have had so much rain. But a few hot sunny days have dried up everything. Then I'd like you to run up to the shop for me."

The breakfast things cleared away and washing up over, Cyril fixed the hose to the tap and then departed on his shopping errand.

The good lady was thoughtfully watering a bed of strawberries when her attention was caught by the loud chirping of a flock of sparrows that came swooping over the back fence, chattering at the top of their voices. She glanced at them in wonder as they swept to a landing on a patch of lawn not six feet from her. They were squabbling over something on the ground, but she could not discern what it was.

"Oh, be quiet, you noisy things!" she exclaimed and swung the hose on them. Immediately their chattering changed to indignant squawks and the whole band of six flew away over the back fence again.

And then Mrs. Gorton saw what they had been fighting with. Uttering a cry of alarm, she threw the hose aside and ran across the lawn—to stoop down and pick up a canary. As it lay, moving feebly, in the palm of her hand, tears gathered in her eyes and she gave way to a very rare burst of anger.

"Oh, those useless, awful sparrows!" she cried piteously. "What have they done to you, you poor little thing! Oh, I could kill every sparrow on the face of the earth!" Forgetting the hose, which was shooting water all over the place, she hurried inside, spread out a soft towel on the kitchen table and examined the canary closely. The breed, she saw at once, was Border Fancy. It was a plain yellow bird with a black spot as big as threepence on the back of its head and a touch of buff on one wing. Its feathers were wet and bedraggled and there was a faint splash of blood under one eye. With fingers as gentle as thistledown, she felt the little body all over. The heart was beating faintly.

"It has had a bad shock and is in a fainting fit," she murmured. "It does not appear to be bodily injured. Oh, I must save the poor little mite, but I can do nothing until it regains consciousness."

Quickly she went to the cupboard and secured a deep dish. This she inverted over the bird to prevent it from escaping should it recover before she had made her hospital preparations. Then she left the house and ran to the shed at the bottom of the yard where she had several empty cages. Hastening back to the kitchen with a small clean one, she removed the dish and gently picked up the canary, which was showing signs of returning animation. She opened the cage door, placed the folded towel on the floor and then laid the canary on it. Then she took the cage into her own bedroom, placed it in a corner and covered it with a cloth.

"Peace and quiet. That is what it wants for a few hours to recover from its fit."

Closing the bedroom door softly, she returned to the yard and went on with the watering. Her mind was not on it. With a sigh she turned the tap off and returned to the bedroom. A quick inspection of the cage showed that the canary was now crouched in a corner. Its eyes were half-opened and it was breathing heavily.

Mrs. Gorton sighed with relief. If its trouble was merely a fainting fit, it would soon recover. In the meantime, she would prepare a meal for it. An iron tonic and some plain seed. That was what it needed. And that was what it got. She left the cage in the quiet room and forced herself to stay away from it for a whole hour.

When Cyril returned home she gave him full details of what had happened, and together they went into the room and inspected the bird. Cyril carried the cage to a table where he could see it properly. Mrs. Gorton was overjoyed to note that the canary was wobbling unsteadily on a perch, while seed scattered around the floor of the cage showed that it had been eating. Cyril, who knew almost as much as his mother about canary ailments, voiced the opinion that the bird had inflammation.

"And, by jove, mother," he exclaimed, peering closely at the bird, "I am certain that this is the same canary that we trapped when we were camping out. I know it by the black spot on the back of its head and the buff marking on the wing. Poor little bird! It has been wandering around in the bush for more than a week and must be half-starved after eating unsuitable food. It is a wonder that it has survived for so long."

Mrs. Gorton had looked bleak at the mention of the camping affair, but she relaxed as Cyril went on talking.

"It must have had an awful time," he said. "No doubt it got out of its cage or was freed by somebody during the floods. I wonder just how many poor little birds that happened to? Most of them would be dead by now—drowned by falling into the water, killed by cats, or hawks, or butcher birds or those useless sparrows, or just died of starvation. It is a terrible thought, isn't it, mother?"

"Yes, my boy, it is," she replied, tears gathering in her eyes as she thought of her own beloved pets. "However, Cyril," she went on in a more cheerful voice, "this little man is in good hands now and we will save him. I agree with you that he might have inflammation. Eating the wrong food and drinking dirty water would cause that. Well, you and I know how to cure that. A cage in a nice warm place, plenty of bread soaked in milk, no seed or green food, and a good tonic. He will soon be back on his feet again."

"I'm sure of that," agreed Cyril. "And I cannot help thinking what a lucky little bird he is."

And Boofie, could he have understood what Cyril was saying, would have agreed with him wholeheartedly. He was a lucky little bird—lucky to he alive.

He had been wandering aimlessly around ever since that morning, three days since, that the owl had killed the glider possum. Food had been scarce—very scarce.

Leaving the bush, he had at last flitted in easy stages back to the outskirts of the township and he was perched on the front fence of a house when he heard the old familiar whistling of one of his own kind. It came from the verandah of the house. The canary was in a cage hanging from a chain and Boofie flew across to it. On the floor under the cage was a quantity of seed carelessly thrown out by the bird, and Boofie thankfully devoured it. The sudden appearance of a huge black cat, which jumped on to the verandah and sprang towards him, sent him shooting into the air again. The cat had not known the canary was on the verandah floor when he leaped on to it, so had shown no caution. Thus Boofie had seen him and was well away before the cat could reach him.

Boofie shot straight across the street and came to rest on the fence of the house opposite. He was sitting there uncertainly when the flock of sparrows descended upon him. These cheeky birds had alighted on the fence on either side of him and had buffeted and pecked at him until, in sheer desperation, he had pecked back. The sparrows took exception to this and began to get really tough.

Taking refuge in his wings, Boofie had flown down the side of the house and over the back fence, where the sparrows had forced him to the ground and were about to deal with him rather harshly when Mrs. Gorton turned the hose on them.

Good food and tender care worked wonders with Boofie and within a week he was as sprightly alert as he ever had been back in his pre-flood days.

And then, early one morning as Mrs. Gorton was feeding the flock, she heard the click of the side gate and observed two small children shyly entering. They paused as they saw her.

"Yes, children, what is it you want?" she called out in a kind voice.

"Please, Mrs. Gorton," said the eldest, a boy of eleven, "my sister and I would like to buy a canary from you if you have any for sale."

"Well, now, children, I don't know that I have," she said slowly, and then permitted herself to tell a lie. "Apart from the ones I desire to keep for myself, all the rest are ordered."

At that statement the faces of both children fell visibly, a fact that the kind-hearted woman did not fail to observe.

"Come along in, anyway, and have a look at them," she invited, and the children eagerly accepted the invitation. "You want a canary for a pet, do you? What are your names? Do you live here? How did you know I owned canaries?"

"A man told us you sold them," spoke up the little girl. "My name is Mary Westwood, and this is my brother, Jacky. We lived over on the river flats on our farm until the floods came. We did have a dear pet canary before the floods, but daddy was trapped on the roof of our hayshed with it and let it out of its cage to give it a chance. Daddy did not think he would be rescued. That is why he let it out. And he was rescued by a Duck not long afterwards. We do miss our little bird."

There were tears in the child's eyes as she finished speaking, and they touched the heart of the kind old lady.

"I'm sure you loved your little bird very much," she said. "Now, maybe, I *could* find a pet for you among all my birds."

"Oh, if you only could!" cried the girl, her eyes dancing with hope. "We would be so good and kind to it. It would always remind us of our poor lost Boofie!"

"Boofie?"

"That is what Dad named our bird because he, er, was, well, er, always doing silly things," she stammered, colouring slightly.

"Canaries can do silly things," smiled Mrs. Gorton. "I have one that I call Terry, who is, I am afraid, quite mad."

She laughed as she said it, and the children laughed with her.

"But come along and have a look at my birds," she went on. "See this cage here? That contains the ones I have for sale. How do you like them?"

"Oh, they are all beautiful!" cried Mary Westwood. "Don't you think so, Jacky?"

"You bet," replied her brother, and as Mary and Mrs. Gorton examined the cage of young birds, he strolled around to have a look at the rest.

Suddenly the others were startled by a loud shout. Jacky was standing in front of a small cage and excitedly pointing at its feathered occupant.

"Mary!" he yelled. "As sure as eggs, it's Boofie! Come and have a look! It's Boofie!"

"O-o-o-o-o-r!" screamed the girl and dashed to his side. One glance at the startled canary was sufficient for her.

"Yes, it is, it is, it is!" she called out, dancing up and down and clapping her hands. "It's our own Boofie! Oh, gee, the darling!"

Wonderingly, Mrs. Gorton inquired what all the excitement was about, and when she could get some sense out of the youngsters they told her that the bird in the cage, the canary with the black spot on the back of his head and the buff on his wing, was Boofie, the bird they thought had been lost in the floods.

Greatly touched, Mrs. Gorton told them how the canary had come into her possession. Their young faces clouded over as they heard about the cruel sparrows, and they listened very seriously as Mrs. Gorton described how she had brought Boofie back to health after his adventures.

Impulsively, Mary Westwood seized her hand and squeezed it.

"Gee, you are a wonderfully kind lady," she said, and there was a sob in her voice. "You are an angel." The good lady turned away for a moment to hide her emotion and then, without saying a word, she lifted the cage down from the wall.

"My dear child," she said simply, "please take this. It is yours.

Boofie, of course, belongs to you. The cage is a gift from an old woman who is not an angel, but who tries to be kind and who does love birds very much. I hope you will accept it."

The girl could hardly speak for a moment. Then, "Thank you very much," she said. "It will stay with us as long as it lives. And you are really, truly an angel. Thank you again."

"I'll say," echoed her brother.

Mrs. Gorton let the two happy children out through the side gate and closed it behind them. And as they walked down the street, the little girl carrying the precious cage and its more precious occupant, the good lady smiled. There were tears in her eyes, but a great joy in her heart.

She watched them until they turned a corner and were lost to sight. Then she walked slowly back to her cages, to be greeted by a chorus of happy songsters, whose lovely melodies, in her humble opinion, far transcended the finest works of the world's most eminent composers.

For, were not those glorious bird melodies the compositions of the Greatest Composer Himself?

AUTHOR'S FINAL CHIRP . . .

The story of Boofie does not end here, though his adventures, I hope, do. If I can prevent it, he will go roving no more. He is too old, for one thing, and more than a trifle cranky.

For Boofie exists in real life, and I own him now. He came into my possession much in the same manner as Mrs. Gorton got him in this story.

My daughter, Elaine, owned a canary, bought from a dealer who described it as "a first-class whistler and a cock bird supreme." This fraud of a bird, who my daughter named "Sweetie," turned out to be a hen, and she was sitting silent in her cage on the rear wall of my home, when Boofie blew in. He came from out of nowhere, flying into the yard while my wife was hosing the garden. She saw him, and thinking that it was "Sweetie" out of the cage, promptly turned the hose on him. He was unable to fly away because of his wet feathers, so my wife pounced on him and, going to the cage, found "Sweetie" still in residence. Boofie joined her and, in due course, became her mate.

That was five years ago. Now, in this year of grace 1956, Boofie is a great-grandfather. He turned me into a canary breeder in a modest way. He got his name because of his peculiar carryings-on. He would never whistle if anyone were looking at him. He lives in solitary state in his own special cage because he detests company and is now too old for breeding. He had to be taken from the community cage because of his gentle habit of beating up all his friends and relations. But he is still the sweetest whistler of the lot—when he is not being watched.

Where the old boy came from, I do not know, but as there was a flood on at the time. He may have been a refugee. The most interesting part of the whole story, however, is that a neighbour of mine, Mr. Max King. An ex-Maitlander like me, actually secured from me for his sister, a son of Boofie to replace a canary she lost in the February 1955 Maitland floods.

As for Boofie himself, I would not part with that eccentric old lad for all the seed in the bird shop.—C.K.T.

THE END

Months after this story had been written, a remarkable coincidence made Boofie's life story complete. A neighbour of mine and a former Maitland resident, Mr. Max King, bought from me two of Boofie's sons. One he still has himself—but the other, named "The Baron," he gave to his sister, who lives in Maitland, to replace a pet actually lost in the disastrous February 1955 floods.

Truly, fact is stranger than fiction!

www.ingramcontent.com/pod-product-compliance
Lightning Source LLC
Chambersburg PA
CBHW072146020426
42334CB00018B/1909